The Human Dilemma

THE

HUMAN

DILEMMA

HERBERT N. WOODWARD

THE BROOKDALE PRESS

NEW YORK

Standard Book Number: 0-912650-00-1
Library of Congress Catalog Number: 72-172394
Printed in the United States of America by Ray Freiman & Company

Contents

Preface

A GOOD PREFACE, I believe, prepares the reader for the book as a whole by providing him a glimpse at the author's mental processes with some hints about why the book was written and how seriously the author takes himself. Also, a good preface is short.

This book has been hammered out over a span of years into a suggested approach to a philosophy of history. It began with some notes in 1955 that were little more than primordial notions. In 1958, I tackled the project in earnest, and after several drafts it began to take shape. But at that point an intense business career drew me away so that the manuscript lay untouched for almost a decade. It was reexamined in 1968 and during the next years it was rewritten several times more.

Writing this book has been, in the main, a lonely task, because I have relied almost exclusively on my own reading and study for my basic data. My day-to-day life has been and still is far from academe, shut off from the interchange of ideas found in close associations with the intellectual community. Obviously, I have been deeply influenced by my sources; I use them as a springboard. No one else, however, can be blamed for the thesis as a whole.

There is nothing tongue in cheek in this book; it is deadly serious. It attempts, however feebly, to take into account all existence back to the formation of the earth, including man's entire history, and to propose a hypothesis about future directions for our species. The only excuse for this colossal presumption is that the alternative to grasping the total nettle was to do nothing at all.

The evolutionary approach to man's past, as developed in this book, required exposure to many academic disciplines. Of necessity, my knowledge in any single field of study is superficial and my credentials are lacking. Yet, it may have been better not to be deeply involved in any single discipline; I hope this has helped me to see the forest as a whole.

The human race is, I believe, heading into a blind alley unless an escape route is found. The main thrust of this work is to develop that thesis. In that sense, this is a pessimistic book, although I am an optimist by nature. Some of the conclusions are unpalatable, no less to me than to the average reader. Much of our education and upbringing will lead us to object to these conclusions, but to disagree with them is not to disprove them.

In the human world today, there are two dominant trends: the accelerating development of machine technology and the simultaneous rapid proliferation of population. These two interwoven trends, more than any others, shape the world we will inhabit in the future. Growth in our population and in our material skills are themselves extensions of the evolutionary process and must be understood within the context of our whole existence. It is these forces—controllable by man but, in fact, almost out of control—that have speeded up the evolutionary process and created the urgency in our human dilemma.

Man is not a helpless victim of circumstances and can make his own future; therefore, it matters immensely how he sets about solving his problems. The present makes the future by what is done and what is thought. More than any creature before, more than ever before in any century, twentieth-century man can make his future what he wants it to be. This choice may not always be open to him; he may not have the chance again.

What are the future directions possible for mankind? What are the long-term goals that we should be shaping? What are the alternatives for the human race as a whole? Which are possible or feasible? These are questions to which this book is addressed. Most of them concern our life here on earth and the problems that an earthbound human race may face. My argument will show why I believe the earth and even the solar system will ultimately prove too finite for man so that he must plan to move up and out for the long-term benefit of the species.

Whether the proposed plan of escape described in the book is more than a lurid science fiction tale is less important than whether the problem to which it may now seem a far-fetched solution (if a solution at all) will, in fact, become a real one. Although the book is packed with positive assertions about past, present, and future, I am not so foolish as to believe that these are ultimate answers. In extenuation, it is meant to be provocative rather than definitive. It will serve its purpose if it stimulates fresh thinking about earthly problems and ways to solve them.

Having made these disclaimers, I leave you on your own.

H. N. W.

May, 1971

The Human Dilemma

1

Man and Machines

TODAY we talk about ourselves and our world being in the midst of the stream of progress. We take for granted the idea of progress without realizing how new an idea it is. Certain preconditions are necessary before the concept of progress is possible.

First, to have progress of any kind, there must be some evidence of change. If progress is defined as an increase in man's control over his physical environment, or, alternatively, as a broadening of the range of choices that he may make, then except for the last three centuries, the increase or broadening within any single lifetime was too slight to be noticeable as a trend. Because progress is as much a conviction as it is an objective reality, its effective force is much too attenuated when it takes vast periods of time to show significant results. It needs a dynamic feedback of its own. Progress could not be measured without a study of history, and one looks in vain in the histories written before the seventeenth century for any hint of such a trend. Most histories were largely chronicles of kings and battles, as there was scant awareness of the underlying forces that shape events.

Second, one must be aware not only that change is taking place but that it can be brought about or guided by the positive action of man. A number of pervasive concepts had prevented any such awareness: for example, the Greek idea of *Moira* is more than an individual's personal fate; it is the Greek concept that the whole cosmos follows an ineluctable plan. Pervasive through the cosmological concepts of many civilizations was the belief that there had once been a golden age in which man led a happy, wholesome, peaceful life in an idyllic rural world and that only later did he become corrupt and evil. This concept was exemplified in the Christian religion by the belief in the Garden of Eden and the fall of man, who eventually required redemption. We also find it in Rousseau, who believed in the ideal life of the primitive savage, with whom, fortunately, for Rousseau and his beliefs, he had no actual contact. If history is cyclical —whether it be in the sense of the ancient Greek historians or of Oswald Spengler, or of Arnold Toynbee—progress has meaning only if man can break out of the circle. If all the best is in the past and knowledge only corrupts, then progress as we regard it is a positive evil.

Third, a belief that life on this earth is unimportant makes man relatively indifferent to any changes in his condition. The Christian emphasis on the life after death, so like the Egyptian preoccupation with the afterworld, was no stimulus to physical improvement of the world. So long, too, as life for almost all mankind was bitterly cruel, gloomy, and uncertain, demanding almost unremitting toil, the vision of a static, peaceful heaven represented the ultimate in potential happiness. A phantom progress on earth for some future generation had no reality.

The idea of progress, then, as Carl Becker defines it, "the expansion of intelligence and the multiplication of the implements of power" (1949, p. 26), could not have appeared sooner than it did. All three beliefs prerequisite to a recognition of progress first emerged in the scientific Age of Reason.

Lewis Mumford suggests a fourth prerequisite by emphasizing the importance of the clock in modern civilization (taking his clue from Spengler) in helping "to give human enterprise the regular collective beat and rhythm of the machine" (1963, p. 14).

Conscious progress began hardly more than two centuries ago. The expansion of knowledge of the physical world and the wonderful laws that seem to control its operation gave direction to scientific effort. But it was the application of this knowledge to the daily life of man that gave it impetus. The tools that man has created are a measure of his power. Indeed, the physical tools of the practical world are the effective expression of the development of knowledge and abstract thought that must precede and accompany them. This is the way progress is understood.

In talking about man the technician, José Ortega y Gasset divides technology into three periods: technology of chance, technology of the craftsman, and technology of the technician. Technology of chance, commonest in primitive times, occurs when an invention happens by accident and is not the result of a deliberate search for a solution to a prob-

5

lem. By this definition, the ape who puts together a pair of jointed sticks to reach a banana comes upon the solution largely by chance if the components happen to be in front of him at the moment the need arises. The tools of Neolithic cultures were probably invented accidentally. The hunter did not say, "Now I will invent the bow and arrow"; more likely, as he was waiting for his prey, he leaned the butt of his spear against a resilient branch, which, when released, cast it forward. But even here a recognition of the meaning of the accidental discovery is necesssary. This kind of discovery continues today, for many inventions are the result of an accidental concatenation of products or events.

Technology of the craftsman is more than accidental, but it is limited to what can be done with hand tools, which are merely an extension of man's body. Ortega calls it "a definite fund of knowledge not admitting of substantial amplification," because man still supplies all the muscle power and guidance for each such tool he uses. The third stage began, in the opinion of Ortega, with the invention of the weaving machine in 1825. Ortega calls this the first tool that worked by itself to reveal technology as a function entirely independent of natural man, a function that reaches far beyond the bounds set for him.

In the history of technology, the attitude toward technology is as important as the individual inventions are. First, there must be a recognition that something has been discovered: the mind must form a concept: "If we can capture this fire, it will serve us thus and so"; "If we sharpen this ax, it will cut deeper." Next, there must be the willingness to try out the new invention and, if it works, to adopt it as part of the culture. In regard to this, the biggest stumbling block of all, Ortega has something pertinent to say:

> It would be vain to attempt to study technology as though it were an independent entity; it is not directed by a single purpose known to us beforehand. The idea of progress, pernicious in all fields applied without caution, has been disastrous here also. It assumes that man's vital desires are always the same, that the only thing that varies in the course of time is the progressive advance toward their fulfillment. But this is as wrong as wrong can be. The idea of human life, the profile of well-being, has changed countless times and sometimes so radically that definite advances were abandoned, their traces lost. . . . In other cases, and they are almost the most frequent in history, invention and inventor were persecuted as immoral. The fact that we ourselves are urged on by an irresistible hunger for invention does not justfy the inference that it has always been thus. On the contrary, more often than not, man has had a mysterious horror of discoveries, as though he felt lurking under their apparent beneficence the threat of a terrible danger. And we, amid all our enthusiasm for technical inventions, are we not beginning to experience something similar.*

Today, it is taken for granted that inventions are to be put to use. After the Age of Reason, the faith in progress ensured the ready reception of every discovery that would

---

*From José Ortega y Gasset, *Toward a Philosophy of History,* Helene Weyl (trans.) (New York: Norton, 1941), p. 102, by permission of the publisher. Copyright 1932 by W. W. Norton & Company, Inc. Copyright renewed © 1960 by Teresa Carey.

augment man's power over his physical world. The temperament of Western civilization is unlike that of any other civilization we know. We cannot yet tell whether this eagerness for what is new and different marks it as a sport among civilizations, or whether this spirit will die with Western culture.

Opposition to technological progress is never buried very deep. Resistance to change takes many forms, but is usually expressed by those with vested interests; they see no merit in rocking the boat. The objection of sacrilege has been raised more than any other, and established religions, which derive their strength from the protection of the status quo, have voiced the objections of countless gods whom they deem to be equally interested in preserving ancient ways. "God does not intend that we should know or do these things" has been the excuse for opposing almost everything new from the theories of Copernicus to the use of umbrellas.

In the last 300 years, one of the few periods of free thought in all human existence, these voices have been submerged, although not entirely silenced. Today, as the mechanical creatures that man is building take on more of the aspects of Frankenstein's monster, the voices are beginning to be heard again.

The scientific discoveries of the sixteenth and seventeenth centuries set the stage for the Industrial Revolution. When machines began to function on their own, while the machine-tender stood by and watched, they triggered a change in man's thinking about himself. He became conscious that he could mold his own destiny. He is still aware that his power is puny and his life short, and he knows better than ever how insignificant he is in the scheme of the universe. But his Faustian willfulness and insatiability is more evident than ever in his desire to do more than discover, his insistence that he must create his own life and his own future. He feels that he is, at least to some degree, master of his destiny.

The Industrial Revolution was given its impetus by the discovery of steam power. Invention followed invention. Steam power, electric power, atomic power, each speeded up the pace of life. The pyramiding advances in technology released more and more bodies from the crushing toil of poverty and more and more minds were working to push progress on faster and faster. Many felt (and still feel) that we are moving too fast, that our knowledge of things was outrunning our ability to use them, that we had to stop while there was still time and learn first to control our own natures. Our learning has been admittedly one-sided: we understand how a distant star burns, but we know next to nothing about how our own brains function; we are adept at moving physical mountains but we cannot overcome stupidity and venality in our midst.

A few recognized the forces that were at work and understood that there could be no turning back. Henry Adams said it over 60 years ago, and his foresight contrasts sharply with the conservatism of most of the other thinkers of his day:

. . . if he [Adams] had, at times, felt serious differences with the American of the nineteenth century, he felt none with the American of the twentieth. For this new creation, born since 1900, a historian asked no longer to be teacher or even friend; he asked only to be a pupil, and promised to be docile, for once, even though trodden under foot; for he could see that the new American—the child of incalculable coal-power, chemical power, electric power and radiating energy, as well as of new forces as yet undetermined—must be a sort of God compared with any former creation of nature. At the rate of progress since 1800, every American who lived into the year 2000 would know how to control unlimited power. He would think in complexities unimaginable to an earlier mind. He would deal with problems altogether beyond the range of an earlier society. To him the nineteenth century would stand on the same plane with the fourth—equally childlike—and he would only wonder how both of them, knowing so little and so weak in force, should have done so much.*

Scientific and technological advance in the past century has been greater and faster than the best scientific and technical minds have anticipated. Only since World War II have we had a more general recognition that the actual rate of discovery both in pure science and practical technology is climbing rapidly. In many fields more progress has been made in the last decade than in the previous quarter-century and the previous twenty-five years' accomplishment exceeded that of the whole century that preceded it.

Why is this so? Without trying to measure their relative importance or even claiming an inclusive list, these are the reasons I consider most important:

1. Each new idea and invention becomes part of our permanent intellectual capital, and once completed, the dis-

*From Henry Adams, *The Education of Henry Adams* (Boston: Houghton Mifflin, 1918), pp. 496–497, by permission of the publisher.

coverer or inventor is released to work on a different project, so that we have a kind of compound interest working for us.

2. Many new discoveries in the fields of pure science have practical applications that raise the standard of living enough to free more people to work in pure science.

3. In lengthening the average human life, medical science has increased the productivity of the individual by stretching out his middle productive years, without adding to the cost of educating and training him.

4. Many practical technical tools developed by industry are used by pure scientists to speed or improve their research and in some cases such tools help to open up entire new fields of study.

5. Improvement in the technology of communications has had a secondary effect; it speeds up the transmission and dissemination of information on new discoveries to all those who may learn or benefit from them, so that the lag between discovery and application, or between discovery and the next step of discovery, is being reduced.

6. The development of machines such as the whole range of computers to do all kinds of advanced thinking not only opens new possibilities but cuts down the time between steps in the discovery process.

7. The increased speed and efficiency of organized scientific research by producing more results in shorter time has encouraged the expenditure of more and more effort and funds for additional research at a compounding rate.

8. Competition of all kinds is getting keener every year, putting more pressure on science and industry to produce better goods faster.

9. The competitive military situation in the world has stimulated research by governments in many fields in which private industry could not justify giant costs for commercial exploitation only. Notable among these are the Manhattan Project in atomic energy and the present varied space projects.

10. Finally, as the pace of progress increases, there is growing awareness of its impetus, and more of us, caught up in the excitement of seeing the world go faster and faster, thus become eager to give it a push ourselves.

In today's world, it is one short step from idea to actuality. Only 20 years ago the miracle machines already serving us today were almost inconceivable. The pace of acceleration of discovery is breathtaking. The new inventions that tumble upon us seem always to catch us unawares. We receive a hint of a new invention to which we pay little attention, and then all of a sudden it becomes an everyday reality, and soon we forget how life was carried on before it came.

Why are the prophets so far off on the time required? There is probably no single reason. Scientists and professional scholars are naturally conservative. They are close to the problems of their work and are immersed in the obvious difficulties to be overcome. They project the results of their efforts in a straight line instead of an ascending curve, still not quite realizing the ascending rate of technological progress. They are unwilling to anticipate major breakthroughs in invention or discovery, because there is no basis for predicting them.

Major breakthroughs do occur, however, and although

we cannot predict what they will be, we can be quite sure that they will occur, and often. The unexpected must be expected. In this increasingly complex world, even the most catholic of scientists can know only the surface of information available outside his special field, and he is unlikely to anticipate the cross-fertilization of ideas that will occur between distant fields of learning.

Will progress in man's control over his own future continue indefinitely? This is a very different question. It is apparent from even a casual glance at the evolutionary history of life on earth that no single formula explains all change. We assign weight to different forces affecting our lives only at our peril. Man is now rapidly mastering still other aspects of his physical environment. Unless he blows himself up, however, I see no present tendency to apply brakes to this rocketing pace.

In this delicately balanced world economy superimposed on a complex biological ecology, we can be sure that changes in direction will occur. The entire 6,000 years since civilization began is only 1/500,000 part of the 3 billion years since life began on earth. Most of these changes have occurred in the very last of these 6,000 years.

The machine world is impinging on our lives in myriad ways. In the last few years in particular, we have become accustomed to new ideas and new machines butting into our conscious vision with increasing frequency. These machines are doing all kinds of amazing things. What new wonders may we expect tomorrow? How far will this machine age go? Machines are steadily eliminating the toil of life; may we expect that some day man need not work at all? These are not foolish questions; they must be taken seriously now.

Take the question first in its extreme form: May we expect that man will be able to build machines that will do everything that he or present machines now do to support him at his present or at a higher standard of living; will he become a completely superfluous free rider on the economy? Would this be the logical terminal point of this progress explosion? This is first a technological question, rather than an economic, political, or social one.

Starting in the nineteenth century with the automatic loom in the textile industry, a host of highly specialized machines were built to perform single or complex operations requiring only a machine-tender, whose job is to stand by to load the machines with raw material and to forestall or repair machine breakdowns. Initially, each of these individual operations was treated as a job, and a lot or batch was run and then set aside until the schedule called for the next machine (or sometimes the same machine) to perform the next operation.

But in certain industries it was found possible to link a number of operations together in a single process and run the whole series of operations continuously. The steel industry with its continuous blast furnace and the petroleum industry with its continuous fractionating plants are notable examples. In many processes, human beings acted as the specialized machines, as on the automobile assembly line, where the workers, each with a highly specialized job to do, swarm over the auto as it moves down the conveyor.

In the production of goods in high volume for the masses, the division of labor is being carried close to its practical ultimate. Many workers' days are devoted to the repetitive

14

performance of a single miniscule operation on a single un-changing product. In the United States, where mass produc-tion has reached its peak, many of the nation's goods are still produced by human laborers performing such special-ized and usually unskilled operations.

Fundamental to automatic production is the concept of the interchangeability of parts. No two parts are or can ever be exactly alike. The goal is to make all the individuals in a collection of any given part similar enough within certain tolerances so that any one of the batch of parts selected at random will slip into place in the whole product. This elimi-nates hand-fitting. Although interchangeability was com-mon in many industries shortly after the turn of the century, hand-fitting in the assembly of many products survived until World War II, as, for example, in the assembly of the higher-priced automobiles. During the war, when different parts of a weapon were made in different plants around the United States, these parts had to be made accurately enough so that they would fall together at the assembly plant without hand-fitting. Therefore, tolerances were set for each dimension of every part close enough to insure fall-together fit. This concept, once painfully learned by American industry, proved so much more economical that it is now standard in all machined work.

In the last two decades, new forces have been at work. The field of electronics has opened up possibilities scarcely dreamed of a few years ago. Where automatic operations are being performed, electronic controls can be attached to the machine, thus eliminating the need for the machine-ten-der. These controls will check for errors in the product, reject and remove defective parts, and check and correct the machine settings to ensure uniform quality within allowable tolerances.

Not all production operations are in high volume. In the largest economies, many products are made in very small quantity—for example, the machines themselves that make the products the consumer uses. It does not pay to build highly specialized single-purpose tools to perform a single operation on an item when only a handful will be needed. New knowledge of electronics, however, permits us to build complex controls for general purpose machinery that will set up and perform an operation or a series of operations on a single piece in less time than it takes a skilled toolmaker or machinist to begin to plan how he will go about it. These inventions, it is true, impinge only fragmentarily on our industrial economy today, but will soon be used much more.

Manufacturing is, of course, only part of the economy. This same mechanization is taking place in almost all fields including distribution, finance, transportation, construction, and agriculture. Most improvements have been aimed at reducing the need for unskilled or semiskilled labor in all fields. This type of work is the simplest and most repetitive, and therefore the easiest to mechanize economically. Inventive attention has also been centered on the jobs where the very power of the machine far exceeds the strength of man's shoulders and back, as dramatically shown in modern earth-moving equipment. Finally, it is also being concentrated on performing all kinds of wonders to expand and enrich our lives that could be done in no other way.

As a percentage of the total labor force in the United States, unskilled workers are on the decline whereas professional, technical, and managerial personnel are on the rise. The machine is taking over more of the unskilled work, so that with a constant total level of employment, the standard of living rises as new mechanical "slaves" are added. One could guess that the average servantless American is far better served than an ancient Greek with an entourage of 50 slaves to do his bidding.

Many kinds of work are still not done by machines. For our purpose, these may be divided into three categories. First, a multitude of jobs could be done by machine but we have just not yet built enough of them. If all our most modern equipment were in use everywhere, ignoring any ideas still on the drawing board, life would have far less drudgery and show a giant gain in convenience, scope, and beauty. There is a natural lag between invention, production, and widespread use; millions of families in the United States still do not have powered refrigerators, for example.

Second, machines could be designed and built to do countless jobs that cannot (and may never be) justified by economics; jobs for which human labor is still faster, more flexible and adaptable, less cumbersome, and (most crucial of all) less expensive. As time goes on, however, many jobs move from the second category to the first, partly because the cost of human labor increases but also because better and more efficient machines are developed. The automatic elevator has been in use for decades, but only in recent years has it been good enough to replace the human operator in the giant office buildings, and only because electronic programming has become economically feasible. A machine could be designed to take the household dishes out of the dishwasher and put them back in the cupboard, but such a machine would not be economically feasible at the present time. Machines are doing more of life's difficult chores, but the human hand is still used for the minor operations not yet worth mechanizing.

Third, many jobs need doing for which we can presently visualize no machine with the capacity to do them. Eventually all the routine operations may become mechanized, but the nexus of creative thought, planning, administration, artistic endeavor, and organization will still remain. How much of this work may machines some day do? (The very special place of the computer in the future advance of technology will concern us in Chapter II.)

No immediate reason is known why all these forces will not continue to operate with increasing speed and power. If man can change himself and rebuild his own personality half as well as he can develop new tools to conquer his environment, his future is assured—provided he does not sacrifice his restless drive which is his most painful and most precious heritage.

It is idle to discuss the kind of lives our technology will permit us to lead 30 or 40 years from now. It is superficial to talk about the new technological developments that will then make life pleasanter and more interesting: automatic kitchens, three-dimensional television, incredibly high-speed travel, and so on ad infinitum; the changes will be greater and deeper. Discussing only specific products that may be expected to enrich our lives gives only a minimal projection of certain aspects of present technology at present rates of improvement. Change will not happen that way. All life will be different, not just isolated segments of our material existence. Suddenly, our knowledge and disciplines are simultaneously breaking new ground, and their interaction will affect us in ways that cannot be anticipated.

With almost unlimited power within our grasp, we will be able to move mountains or oceans, regulate the weather to suit our convenience, jolt the earth out of its orbit if desirable, eliminate all the species that do not serve us as we would be served, and empty the horn of plenty on all the peoples of the world. We will be able to do almost everything we choose to do, not slowly and painfully but on a moment's notice. This is within our technological capacity; whether we do it depends on how we cope with the biological, social and political forces that have at least equal influence on our future.

2

The Brain and the Computer

CAN machines be built that duplicate most or all the functions of the human mind? Little is known about our minds. Much is being learned about the functioning of the brain, but many steps in the process elude analysis. It is immensely complex; there are about 12 billion cells, each an incredibly complicated entity, in the thinking part of the brain. It is a message center like a giant telephone exchange, but it does much more than transmit messages; it receives, edits, interprets, suppresses, and coordinates the information pouring in, and it originates messages on new subjects that seem unrelated to the mass of material it is receiving. In addition, it is a giant memory storage unit, able to store not just impressions but meanings and to draw upon them as needed. More than that, it is, as J. A. V. Butler says, "an organ of continuity" with a constant feedback of present experiences into the record of the past so that it is "permanently modified by every operation . . . performed" (1959, p. 147).

Sir Charles Sherrington's word picture of the brain awakening from sleep is a vivid one:

> In the great head-end which has been mostly darkness spring up myriads of twinkling stationary lights and myriads of trains of moving lights of many different directions. It is as though activity from one of those local places which continued restless in the darkened main-mass suddenly spread far and wide and invaded all. The great topmost sheet of the mass, that where hardly a light had twinkled or moved, becomes now a sparkling field of rhythmic flashing points with trains of travelling sparks hurrying hither and thither. The brain is waking and with it the mind is returning. It is as if the Milky Way entered upon some cosmic dance. Swiftly the head-mass becomes an enchanted loom where millions of flashing shuttles weave a dissolving pattern, always a meaningful pattern though never an abiding one; a shifting harmony of subpatterns. Now as the waking body rouses, subpatterns of this great harmony of activity stretch down into the unlit tracks of the stalk-piece of the scheme. Strings of flashing and travelling sparks engage the lengths of it. This means that the body is up and rises to meet its waking day. (Sherrington, 1955, p. 184)

If machines are ever to be built to duplicate a substantial part of these functions, it is well to be aware of the sheer size of the problem. Studies of the lowly insect-eating bat show how much we still have to accomplish before any ma-

chine even approximates the brain of a bat! Certain species
of these bats that fly in near or total darkness have evolved
a sonar system for flying without the aid of vision and
catching their daily ingest of insects without ever seeing
their prey. The bats obtain a fairly detailed acoustic picture
of their surroundings by means of echo location. This requires a truly remarkable discriminator that detects prey despite all kinds of other noises which amount to jamming.
The bats send out high-pitched sonar signals while cruising
through a cave, changing the wave length of the signal as
they close in, to suit the size of the object pursued. The
echoes are about 1/2,000 the strength of the sounds being
sent out, and the bat must pick out and interpret these
echoes in a field as loud as the emitted sound. What a feat
of auditory discrimination! The whole system is packed into
a tiny part of the bat brain, which weighs not over a half-
ounce (Griffin, 1958, p. 40).

Donald Griffin stated that if the bat's sonar relative
efficiency is considered to be 1, then the efficiency of the
best man-made sonar then (1958) made was 10^{-12}
(.000000000001). How far our mighty machines must go before they can match a small part of the brain of a bat, which
has had 50 million years of evolution in which to refine itself. The difference, however, between 1 and 10^{-12} is composed of two factors: one is the superior sensitivity of the
bat sonar to do a specific job, and the other is the compara-
tive size of the necessary equipment. Although the bat
sonar brain is highly refined and does a most delicate job
with greater flexibility than its mechanical counterpart, man
could probably build as sensitive a machine if needed. Such

a machine would be bulky, but it is not always necessary that we match the compactness of the biological organ to get the job done (although weight would be vital if the machine had to chase insects).

In the ten years since Griffin's experiments with bats, however, miniaturization of electronic componentry has progressed beyond our wildest dreams. These developments are summed up by Richard Landers:

> Consider the following statement made in 1954 by the neurophysiologist John H. Troll: "The human memory is a filing system that has a far greater capacity than that of the largest thinking machine built. A mechanical brain that has as many tubes or relays as the human brain has nerve cells (some ten billion) would fit into the Empire State Building, and would require the entire output of Niagara Falls to supply the power and the Niagara River to cool it. Moreover, such a computer could operate but a fraction of a second at a time before several thousand of its tubes would fail and have to be replaced."
>
> . . . When Troll expressed his opinion in 1954, the relatively large vacuum tube was the primary functional component used in computers. Using transistors, the same computer of ten billion human-like parts would take only one floor of the Empire State Building. However, the current third generation of computers use integrated circuits which, to continue our analogy, would require only a small office of the Empire State Building. Carrying the miniaturization process a step further, current technology indicates component densities enabling 10 billion computer parts—which are essentially on-off switches—to be packaged in a drawer of a desk.

Regarding smaller packages, the field of cryogenics can yield even smaller packaging possibilities . . . allow[ing] packaging billions of units in a cube that measures one tenth of one inch. John von Neumann once calculated that electronic cells could be ten billion times more efficient than biological cells (they are already one million to ten million times faster in operation).*

In respect to complexity, therefore, we are at the point where we can seriously compare the living brain with a machine and establish a mathematical relationship between them. But can a machine think? That question prompts strong emotional reactions. It is commonly said that although machines can be built to perform amazing feats, they can never be made to think, because a machine can do no more than is put into it. This argument is supposed to prove that man's uniqueness can never be duplicated. If, by definition, only man can have conceptual thoughts, then obviously a machine cannot.

But the words "thinking" and "thought" are vague and ill defined, and, include many degrees and kinds of mental processes. In many senses, machines do "think" now. An analog computer that can analyze the course of a missile approaching our country and work out the best interception course for an antimissile missile is doing more thinking than most of us could, even if we didn't have to do it in a fraction of a minute. Any person who attempted this task would feel that he had been thinking very hard, even though all the data was supplied to him.

---

*From the book *Man's Place in the Dybosphere* by Richard Landers © 1966 by Prentice-Hall, Inc. Published by Prentice-Hall, Inc., Englewood Cliffs, New Jersey. From pp. 149–151.

Digital computers have been programmed to play increasingly respectable games of chess—a game that requires at each move an analysis of the player's possible moves, of his opponent's possible countermoves, of his own possible countermoves following each such possible opponent's move, and so on for a number of moves ahead, as well as an evaluation, based on this analysis, of the best move under the circumstances. It is estimated that there are some 10^{120} possible different chess games. To give significance to this figure, note that if the machine could play 1 million games per second, it would take 10^{108} years to play all the possible combinations. (The number of atoms in the entire visible universe out to the farthest galaxy is somewhere about 10^{80}.) Therefore—and this is the most important point—the machine cannot pick the best answer because, like the human brain, it is able to consider only a few of the possible courses of action and must exercise a form of judgment in picking a good course of action against its opponent.

A digital computer reacts mechanically and automatically; although it chooses among a number of courses of action, given exactly the same set of circumstances, its reaction will always be the same. But the more complex the machine becomes, the more circumstances it can take into account; and thus, with increasing complexity, the likelihood of stereotyped response declines. The programming of some of these machines includes a feedback mechanism that records the results of its various moves in its core storage (artificial "memory"), so that the machine will benefit from its own experience and avoid making the same wrong move twice. As the machine becomes more complex, provision can be made for keeping a record of the styles of play of its various opponents so that it can forecast the possible moves its opponents will make and thus counter them more effectively. Today it is acknowledged that within a few years a computer will become unbeatable at chess except by another computer.

Simultaneously with the development of increasingly sophisticated computers, biologists and physiologists are learning more about how the human brain functions. These two lines of study are on a converging course. In recent years, particularly in connection with various probes into outer space, we hear that "redundancy" has been built into a device to insure its success despite failure of some of the components. That is, for each essential function of the device, more than one set of controls has been provided so that if one set is knocked out, the other is available to prevent mission failure. We are becoming increasingly aware of how much redundancy has been built into the human brain.

A machine called the Perceptron, developed at Cornell University Aeronautical Laboratories, illustrates this convergence, because the machine was built to simulate more closely than other computers some of the processes of the human brain. Most of the memory cells of the Perceptron's "nervous system" are wired randomly in contrast to the storage cells of an ordinary electronic computer which are connected in a precise pattern. Almost all the memory cells of the Perceptron react when information is received; the machine does not have a separate memory cell to store each bit of information. The structure of the Perceptron conforms with generally accepted physiological findings that the nerve fibers connecting living sensory and motor systems are organized and can be traced in the body, but are connected randomly through the memory and association cells.

The machine sees its environment through a lens that focuses an image on a "retina" of photoelectric cells. Each image or stimulus activates a portion of the cells. The signal from the activated photocells passes randomly through a portion of the memory cells to reach the response units, one or more of which would be turned on. The memory cells that conducted the signals to the "on" responses are strengthened and their future output signals tend to dominate the output of the other memory cells. An aftereffect or memory trace is created by the relative dominance of the memory cells. During the early part of any learning program, the machine, like a human, tends to make mistakes. But under repeated exposures to the environment, some traces are gradually reinforced. Probability theory shows that certain stimuli will nearly always evoke the same response. When this state is achieved, the machine is said to have reached and evolved certain concepts about its environment.

The Perceptron is the first nonbiological system known to be capable of classifying, conceptualizing, and symbolizing its environment, even a completely new and unanticipated environment, in the absence of human training and control. By comparison, the most modern digital computers can be described as rapid adding machines that work only with the information previously stored in the memory bank. (This discussion of the Perceptron is summarized from an article in *Aviation Week;* see Button, Jr. [1958].)

Although early publicity on the Perceptron may have

made exaggerated claims, the originators of the Perceptron are working in an exciting direction. We know that several thousand neurons die in the human brain every day and yet the brain can function with stability and precision; the whole, because of sufficient redundancy, is more stable than its components. In *Brains, Machines and Mathematics* Michael Arbib points out that in building the Perceptron, it was found that "neither precision nor reliability of the components is important and the connections need not be precise" and that the Perceptron can learn despite "trainer" error (1964, p.45).

A large part of the job of the brain is to receive the flood of information from the senses, identify and classify this information, and route it through the organism to the appropriate decision or action center. The digital computer has no means of obtaining information on its own; it exists in darkness and can only digest what is pressed into its mouth.

Now that the digital computer has the capacity to process the data it receives at unbelievable speeds, machines must be developed that will be capable of feeding the information to it fast enough. Optical scanning machines that read printing directly and even handwriting are now being produced to meet this need. This is a first step toward putting the machine in more direct touch with one aspect of the real world. At the same time, an independent study of the visual system of the frog is proving valuable in understanding how the brain learns from the external world by analyzing precisely how the receptors in the frog's eye report the signals they receive to provide a meaningful pattern to the brain. Now that the groundwork has been done and attention is focused on this field, more rapid progress may be expected.

Whether a machine can "create" something that is not in it when it is built, in the sense in which the word is generally understood, depends upon how complex the machine is. If it has a great enough variety of component responses to the environment to which it is exposed, it will come up with final responses impossible to predict and almost infinite in their variety.

When the relationship between cause and effect is comparatively simple, the reaction is called "automatic" in machines and "instinctive" in animals. Originality or creation seems to occur when the end product cannot be anticipated, even though it could have been deduced as one possible result among many from the data introduced. The difference between a Monet landscape and an orange disk painted by a child to represent the sun is one of degree, although the former is certainly "original" and the latter is probably not.

As machines take over more of the coordinating, planning, and thinking functions—as, for example, in a completely automatic chemical processing plant—they tend to develop personalities of their own. The number of variables being constantly analyzed becomes so great that the thinking process almost defies human ability to find out what really is going on. In biological evolution, a complex organism can develop from a relatively simple one without the intervention of a *deus ex machina*. So man can create and build machines that become learned beyond his own understanding.

The factor of complication in the long-term development of machines was summed up by John von Neumann:

Complication in its lower levels is probably degenerative, that is, that every automaton that can produce other automata will only be able to produce less complicated ones. There is, however, a certain minimum level where this degenerative characteristic ceases to be universal. At this point automata which can reproduce themselves, or even construct higher entities, become possible. This fact, that complication, as well as organization, below a certain minimum level is degenerative, and beyond that level can become self-supporting and even increasing will clearly play an important role in any future theory of the subject. (von Neumann, 1956, p. 2098)

That machines can be built with adequate complexity no longer seems to be in doubt. Nor will it be long before they will be compact enough to produce sufficient mobility, flexibility, and adaptability. Machines, however, have a long way to go before they are able to collect their own data (although machines like the Perceptron are first steps in that direction). Because of this limitation, machines lack what Edmund Berkeley and Lawrence Wainwright call the "elaborate trained judgment of the real world (that) is often an inescapable ingredient for answering a question" (1962, p. 26).

If machines can be made to create or think, then there is no theoretical limit to what they can eventually achieve within the rules laid down by the physical laws of the universe. Although a common argument is that computers can do only what they are programmed to do or have "learned" to do, so are humans largely limited by their inherent capacities as modified by education and training. It is our great complexity that gives us freedom or, perhaps, only the illusion of freedom. As von Neumann pointed out, sufficiently complex machines could have the same attributes.

Emotion is, of course, a necessary factor in our judgment. As a simple example, pain warns us that we are injuring ourselves; thus, the child learns not to touch the hot stove. For the same reason, robots will need feedbacks to warn of self-injury. Our more sophisticated emotions have developed through evolutionary aeons because they help to insure our survival in countless subtle ways. Man has more complex emotions than any other animal. We must assume, then, that the most successful and complex future robot brains will have a circuitry that will perform the same roles. They will need a continuous stream of information about the real world to provide the data for determining alternative courses of action. Depending on the basic interests and goals designed into the machine, the robot will act from this data. When the basic interests and goals are complex, as they will be, deductive reasoning will not be adequate and analogues of human emotional influences will be necessary to arrive at suitable courses of action.

No discussion of machine capabilities is complete without reference to Turing's machine and the so-called Identification Game. In his *Discourse on Method,* Descartes made the point that machines could be made to imitate the form and actions of animals but that no machine could simulate the behavior of man because it could not simulate his power of conceptual thought. A. M. Turing (1950) formalized this Cartesian challenge by setting up precise rules to test this hypothesis. Two human beings and one machine would be placed in separate rooms and communicate with each other only by teletype or by other impersonal means. One person would serve as interrogator and ask any and all questions of the other person and of the machine, without knowing which was which. Both the human being and the machine would be permitted to give false or misleading answers in order to conceal their identities. If the interrogator, after exhaustive questioning, were unable to distinguish between man and machine, then, it might be said that in playing the game successfully the machine had displayed some power of conceptual thought. Such a machine has not yet been built, but we are beginning to see the road that will be followed toward developing one.

The inventor creates machines that can perform tasks better than the human hand. Why else do we use tools? In the same way, the inventor can build computers that perform certain intellectual tasks faster and better than he can do them and (this is important) even if such machines do only what they are told to do. An automobile does only what it is guided to do, but it can still move faster than a man.

Only when we consider the possibility of a machine being superior to us in the higher mental activities do we develop an emotional block, because this possibility cuts to the core of our being. We sigh with relief when we are told that a computer can do only what it is instructed to do. But what if it were instructed to create original concepts and obediently did so. Our relief would disappear and we would recognize that we are playing with words and using them to soothe ourselves.

Is it wise to persist in the argument that only man thinks or is creative? It is a circular argument from false premises and will soon prove as weak a defensive position as the view that the earth was created in 4004 B.C. Man has enough to be proud of without needing false props for his self-esteem. He should rejoice that he is not forever restricted by the vast but still limited capacity of his own mind and that he has the power to create something greater than he is or now can be.

While human beings can cooperate with each other to multiply their effective brainpower, so too can thinking machines be interconnected to multiply their effectiveness. The story of the Central Computer keeps appearing in science fiction stories. The Central Computer is a repository of all the knowledge of the entire culture; it controls the entire economy and keeps it in equilibrium in accordance with a plan that provides for all or almost all contingencies. This is no idle dream, for the ability to create such a machine or combination or machines is almost within our grasp. The awesome moment when machines are able to survive independent of the ministrations of their inventors may not be far distant. With the greater strength and durability possible with metals and ceramics, with the higher speeds and ultimately higher capacities that we can see ahead, the machine world could well outdo and outlast the world of man, it could beat man at his own game.

Research is under way to create machines capable of self-reproduction from their environment. If one machine can build another machine of a different kind, a machine can be designed that will build another in its own image. An early step toward this goal is to design machines that can repair themselves in the event of breakdown. It is only in the final stages of mechanization that all the machines will have to integrate to provide a complete and self-perpetuating organization. It is not surprising that the steps to this ultimate end are still crude. (For an interesting study, see "Self-Reproducing Machines" by L. S. Penrose [1959].)

We must remember that intelligent machines do not have to look human. Most of the robots described in science fiction are crude travesties of human beings; they lurch about with a stiff-legged gait and are meant to inspire condescension. Others, like Rossum's Universal Robots of the play of that name (*R. U. R.*, by Karel Capek), are built so that you cannot tell that they are not human until you dissect them. (For an imaginative picture of robots that evolved on a nuclear-devastated earth, read "Epilogue," a short story in *Time and Stars* [1964], by Poul Anderson). The intelligent machine has to simulate neither human behavior nor human appearance; it can go its own way.

If we wished to prevent the onset of the future robot world, we might, of course, resort to the method of the Luddites of a century and a half ago and smash the machines all over the world before it is too late. But even if we wanted to do so, we would be as ineffective as those roaming English bands that took out the frustrations of early industrialization on the weaving machines that made it possible.

What does the development of these "intelligent" machines mean in relation to the analysis of man's prospects? First, there is no better example of the accelerating pace of technology; it portends total mechanization of our world in the near future, not centuries hence. Second, from a technological point of view, these robots and computers will be in a position to take over the administrative functions of the economy and, if man permits, perhaps even the policy deci-

35

sions. Third, if these machines acquire the capacity to reproduce themselves, they will, in effect, be a new species capable of competing for man's position in the world ecology.
Finally, if humankind achieves a stable, unified world economy, the prospect of a machine takeover, which we now regard with fear, might be quite acceptable to what may become a stagnant dilettante society.

Perhaps these are chimeras. Still, if we continue to be our
dynamic, restless, competitive selves, we have nothing to
fear from such competition. But as I shall attempt to show,
human torpor in a workless world could be our undoing,
unless we break out of the closed system we call the earth.

3

The Tree of Evolution

IF we assume that technology will continue to expand in scope and increase in power at the same accelerating rate that we are now experiencing, we can picture a completely mechanical world in a very few generations. But it is not solely a matter of technology. Biological, economic, social, and political factors also have a decisive influence on the affairs of man. Let us begin with the biological factors, as these are disclosed by the theory of evolution.

Why must we understand evolution? The laws of biological evolution are the corollaries of physical laws disguised by the complexity of organism, and we are all subject to them. Man may take evolution into his own hands—in some ways he already has—but he is still a product of it.

In *The Origin of Species,* published in 1859, Darwin explained that environmental circumstances favor certain variations in the structure of one living creature over those of another. He held that plants or animals born with a variation that gives them an advantage in life are more likely to survive and reproduce so that, assuming that they pass on these favorable qualities to their descendants, over a period of generations the lines containing those individuals that are less well endowed will decline in number and eventually disappear. But Darwin failed to explain why variations appear at all. If all characteristics are inherited and if we all derive from a common ancestry, why are we not all alike? How can an offspring evolve into something different from any of its ancestors?

The followers of Lamarck firmly believed that the child inherited from the parent the characteristics that the parent acquired during its lifetime, but Lamarckism is now almost completely discredited. Biologists assure us that acquired characteristics per se are not inherited.

If we do not inherit the acquired characteristics of our parents, how does variation come about? It took the later development of genetic theory to explain the cause of the differences that do occur. Genes are the submicroscopic particles in the germ cells that are the sole determinants of inheritable characteristics. In sexual reproduction, the two parents have different sets of genes, and the product or offspring has some genetic characteristics derived from each parent. All these characteristics are inherited. Because the two parents have different genes, the child can inherit any one of a great variety of possible combinations.

But this is not variation. Variation occurs because occasionally genes fail to duplicate themselves accurately, thus causing a change or mutation of one or more characteristics in the next generation. Once mutated, the change in the genes is passed on from generation to generation without reverting to the original premutated form; in other words, the mutation breeds true. Mutations provide evolution with the raw material from which natural selection picks the more viable individuals. The great majority of mutations are detrimental in their effect. The greater the effect, of course, the more likely they are to have severely damaging and even lethal impact on the organism. But, among the ones with small or limited effect, an occasional mutation may, under some circumstances, be beneficial; if the mutation is advantageous, the organism inheriting it may multiply to the point that its progeny are favorably selected so that "an additional step of adaptation has been added to the group and, in some cases, the complexity of the organism will have increased a little" (Muller, 1947, p. 29).

It is fortunate, then, that mutations are rare. Chaos would result if they were frequent. Because there appear to be special genes that inhibit the rate of mutation in the other genes, it may be said that natural selection has eliminated those species in which this restraint was not exercised. In different species, the so-called rate of mutation varies from one in two thousand births to a proportion as rare as one in several million.

What causes mutations? Precisely how do they come about? Here we are at the intersection of the physical and the biological world. We now know that mutations are the relatively infrequent quantum jumps between two relatively stable molecular configurations over an energy threshold; the frequency of these jumps is determined by the mathematics of probability as applied to the relative stability of the configurations (reflected in the height of the threshold) and the average energy level of the atom concerned.

Visualize a faucet dripping water into a small trough. From time to time, certain drops of water will bounce higher than others. Occasionally one will bounce high enough, and it will be at the necessary angle to escape the trough entirely, over the energy threshold into a different environment, where it remains. Random molecular action can be seen in the movement of very small particles—in this case, drops of water. Normally it is too subtle for the human eye to observe.

We see, therefore, that the elemental mutation is the effect of a random dislocation of an atom in a molecule to some new position, resulting in a different molecule with a new configuration and new properties. By this means, complexity can arise from simplicity by natural law. If a simple molecule can become a more complex molecule on its own, then it has become something that did not exist before and it can do this without being alive. In effect, it is a nonliving machine that creates.

A modern example of evolution at work has been closely studied in industrial England over half a century. Certain species of mottled brown night-flying moths spend the days resting on tree trunks, relying on their natural camouflage against the bark of the tree to protect them from being seen and eaten by birds. But over large areas in the past century industrial smoke has blackened the trees to an entirely different color; against this dark background the moths are easily seen. Dark varieties that more nearly match the blackened trunks appeared as mutations at about the turn of the century. Experiments proved that the darker moths had a substantially higher rate of survival in the industrially blackened areas. Initially, there were so few of them that it took many generations for their descendants to amount to as much as 10 percent of the total moth population, but once they reached that percentage they continued to thrive so much better than their light-colored cousins that in 15 to 20 more years they had become 90 percent of the total population (Kettlewell, 1959, p. 48).

Only after studying the process of evolution can man's present position on this planet be properly evaluated. The first thing that is apparent is that life developed over an immensely long period. The best present estimates are that the earth is more than 4½ billion years old and that life probably started about 3 billion years ago. Were we to imagine that this length of time could be compressed into 1 year, then the entire recorded history of man (6,000 years) would take place in the last minute of the last hour on December 31.

How did life begin? Little is certain, but astronomers, geologists, and biologists working together have constructed a picture of how it could have happened. After the earth was formed by condensation of some of the gas clouds that became our solar system, it is believed that it had an atmosphere of water, hydrogen, ammonia, methane, and some hydrogen sulfide. Much of the hydrogen escaped permanently into outer space, including the hydrogen that was the product of the photochemical conversion of water. The atmosphere thus became oxidizing, and ammonia was converted into nitrogen and methane into carbon dioxide (Urey, 1952). Carbon has the property of combining with itself and with certain other elements to form large and very complicated molecules. Under the right conditions, with the right kind of atmosphere and with the influence of sunlight, cosmic rays, and perhaps strong electrical discharges from the storms that are believed to have raged over the earth, life eventually occurred.

The word "occurred" is as close as we can get to the truth, because we do not know just how life started. Nor is there a precise definition of what "life" is as distinguished from "nonlife." Certain simple viruses are said to be at the threshold of life, but one is not sure which side they are on. Such viruses multiply prolifically in an appropriate environment, yet in crystalline form they are just chemical compounds. In this and other borderline instances, we find our terminology a semantic trap, and as a result, biologists shrug their shoulders and refuse to say what is life and what is not.

But in this primeval world, carbon compounds grew larger and more complex until, in Jonathan Leonard's words,

the sea became full of a kind of organic soup.

He continues:

. . . The sea probably contained examples of all the compounds that carbon will form with the other available elements. This stuff does not exist in the sea today; it could not exist because living organisms would attack it and destroy it immediately, but in the primitive sea there was no life. So the organic molecules could grow indefinitely.

At last the blind process of chemical combination, repeated hundreds of trillions of times in each micro-second, produced a molecule with an extraordinary property. It could grow by taking other molecules into its structure, and it could reproduce, probably by the simple maneuver of

breaking into two. This molecule was "alive" and a new
and powerful force had appeared on the earth. (Leonard,
1957, p. 248)

With the appearance of something that we may call life,
with the ability to reproduce itself, the process of biological
natural selection became decisive. Those compounds or organisms (who knows which they were?) that were able to
survive and reproduce best, that were not broken up by the
chemical warfare of other competing bits of matter, spread
through the waters of the world. From these first acids, half
life and half nonlife, it was an incredibly long series of steps
to the level of naked genes, which each contain millions of
atoms. Because changes (mutations) appear randomly in
these compounds and most of such changes affect the organism only slightly, a new and more viable combination of
atoms may take many generations to outreproduce its premutated form and become dominant. In the later stages of
evolution, a mutation that provides the individual with a 1
percent better opportunity to survive is an exceptional one
indeed. The melanism in moths discussed above is a rare
example of a mutation worth far more than 1 percent in
survival value, which accounts for its amazingly rapid
spread in terms of evolutionary time.

The single cell is the building block of life. A cell may be
described as a microscopic but highly complicated living
substance, enclosing a nucleus containing an accurately
self-reproducing set of genes.

It is probable that the smallest visible cell contains about a
quarter of a million protein molecules of many kinds and
larger cells many more. Taking the average protein mole-

cule as containing about 20,000 atoms, we see that the smallest independently living units contain something like five thousand million (5,000,000,000) atoms, united into molecules of great complexity and all the molecules organized into a single functioning whole. (Butler, 1959, p. 156)

A long series of minute changes then brought about the first multicellular organisms, which were larger, more complex, and more varied in function than single-celled beings. Somewhere in this stage, animal life began to be differentiated from vegetable life, as the latter waited for its food to come to it, and the former developed bisymmetry (in other words, a head and a tail) and began to move in search of food.

As long as organisms reproduced entirely by cell division there was no death; all life was immortal because the species survived in all its members. But cell division became a practical impossibility in organisms beyond a certain size, and their power to reproduce became limited to a few cells in the organism that contained the template for building a duplicate of the original. The species could now be perpetuated not by dividing up the entire organism and making two organisms out of one, but by passing on the inheritance through the genes alone. Thus, the tiny genes acted as proxy for the whole, passing on to form new life without disrupting the entire form of the organism in the process. In a very real sense, then, each of us does live on in the form of his children; but because after performing his role in the reproductive process he continues his own life as a conscious being with his sense of self fixed in his own brain, he does not think or feel himself to "be" his children.

Each of the cells within us is alive, has a "being" and many of them, like the red and white corpuscles that are free agents in our circulatory system, lead independent lives fully as rich as the life of any single-celled organism.

Can each of us "be" not only ourselves but also a mass of the individual "being" cells of which we are composed? In the ant community, the individual ant is completely subordinated to the welfare of the society as a whole. Can it not be said that all the ants that make up the nest of ants play the same role in the ant hill that the cells play in our body— partly independent, yet subservient to and cooperative with the needs of the whole? The analogy is a fair one because among ants (and all social insects) all the ants of the nest are the offspring of a single individual and each "shares the variations of that parent individual and virtually *is* that individual in an expanded condition" (Herman J. Muller, 1935, p. 100).

In Western civilization, we think of man as having a strong sense of individuality, but we need to be reminded that, much as we cherish this way of thinking about life, it is not the only possible way. No clear dividing line exists between what is part of me and what of me is part of something else. The cells within us live and divide. Some may die, other new ones may grow and divide and yet we, the organism as a whole, have our own being, both longer and in some respects shorter than its component parts. The sponge is notable as a colony of separate animal cells united in a mutually supporting living system. Squeeze certain sponges through a cloth and the component cells will reunite and reintegrate to form a new sponge colony. Which is the unit of life, the whole or the part?

In any line of evolution, after a certain amount of special-
ization, the line tends to stabilize. For example, when an
insect develops a form of body camouflage that approaches
perfection, the species will stabilize as to this characteristic.
As long as the environment remains unchanged (in this case,
the background against which the insect hides), there is
no tendency to change further. If the environment changes,
the species may or may not be able to adapt to it, depending
on the nature and magnitude of the change and the complicated balance of other characteristics that may be affected.
The moth was able to adjust to industrial melanism; the
giant reptiles of the Mesozoic era could not cope with the
exigencies of a colder, dryer climate.

We must remember that extinction is a normal corollary
of evolution. The extinction of the giant reptiles is not an
unusual result of the process of natural selection. The history of evolution is a succession of extinctions along with a
tremendous expansion of a very few types. Of today's living
vertebrates 98 percent trace their ancestry to eight species
of the Mesozoic era, and only two dozen of the tens of
thousands of Mesozoic vertebrates have left any descendants at all. Man should remember that the overwhelmingly
probable future of any species is extinction (Crow, 1959, p.
138).

Mutation provides the material for evolution; natural selection chooses from the material offered; the laws of mathematical probability insure that this is an irreversible process. Evolution is a one-way street. Nothing once done is
undone. Each organism is the end product of an accretion
that goes back through its ancestry to the beginning of life
and even before. Conditions on earth have remained rela-

tively uniform for long periods of time. As a species develops through natural selection, it tends to adapt to these uniform conditions and the special circumstances in which it finds itself; it becomes specialized in its particular environment. Once specialized, however, it will not and cannot revert to a generalized and more widely adaptable form, even if the environment becomes unsuitable for its specialized abilities. New forms of life develop from those more generalized (and, therefore, often more primitive) species that have not been committed irrevocably to a specialized way of life.

The combination of variations by mutation and the operation of natural selection produces this unidirectional effect. Mutations are entirely random in character and may occur in many directions. But they pass through the sieve of natural selection, which retains only the few that help the species to survive better. R. A. Fisher called natural selection "a mechanism for generating an exceedingly high level of improbability" (Dobzhansky [1958], p. 374).

Evolution in a species could theoretically reverse itself and by new mutations gradually retrace the history of its original development, but the probabilities against it happening are immense. This likelihood compares with the statistical probability that all the molecules of gas in a chamber will find themselves in the same half of the chamber at any instant. Irreversibility works like a ratchet to lock in each step ahead as it is made. Although irreversibility makes evolution possible, it also holds problems for the future that concern mankind today.

Because of its random nature, evolution is exceedingly slow. Natural selection is inefficient and results in incredible waste; it is slow to make choices and is short-sighted in those it makes. It does not anticipate future problems; it chooses on the basis of momentary circumstances. But the vast waste is necessary to eventual success. Nature cannot anticipate how the environment will change; thus, if each species rapidly specialized to the precise conditions of its environment as these existed at any particular time, characteristics desirable in the old environment might be fatal in new and different circumstances. Contrariwise, the misfits of the earlier world might prove better adapted to the new environment. Nature uses a shotgun, not a rifle, because although most of the pellets miss the target, it cannot anticipate which few are going to hit.

A preliminary conclusion emerges from the picture of this complex life on earth. There is no need to assign a single meaning to the whole story of evolution. No single thread ties beginning and end together. It is a combination of, and interplay between, an almost infinite number of stories, each dramatic and exciting in its own right. Some of these stories are completed; as for the rest, we do not know which are in the last chapter and which have scarcely begun.

The history of life on earth has been one of confusion and waste, vast proliferation in a thousand directions, groping endlessly up blind alleys, periods of utter stagnation and periods of dynamic activity, but through it all a constant change, growth, and decay; life and death; rise and fall.

Is a direction discernible in this story? The only change consistently in one direction seems to be that toward greater complexity of biological organisms, among which man is the most complex. But this trend is only one of many patterns of movement and change that influence life in this fascinating world. All members of all living species on earth are subject to a constant pushing and pulling of forces in the ecology's delicate balance. The resultant of these forces determines which individuals and which species survive.

Where does man fit into the evolutionary picture? It is understandable that man, looking at the process of evolution, is interested primarily in what it has to say to him. It is hard to avoid an anthropocentric view of life on earth. How much more pleasant it is to assume that man rules the earth because he is unquestionably superior to all other life in every respect, that it was destined thus, and that all other creatures are here merely for his convenience. With that assumption, man could be content in believing that it will go on this way forever and that if he changes at all, it will be for the better.

It was this anthropocentric view that was shattered by the theory of evolution. Far from portraying a stable man-centered world, it tells a story of change and struggle. When the record is examined, it is evident that there was no certainty about the outcome; on the contrary, life might just as well have evolved in any one of an infinite number of ways.

One need only understand a very few of the steps in the evolutionary process to realize how great were the odds against man ever appearing at all. If we are to approach the problems of present-day man with any objectivity, we must remind ourselves constantly that *Homo sapiens* has no assured place in the scheme of things and only appeared as the result of an extraordinary series of circumstances. Most of us are emotionally ill equipped to take seriously the prospect that we, as a species, might disappear from the earth and yet we must admit this possibility, at least at the intellectual level, if we are to face the future squarely.

All things are constantly changing, and there is no reason why the process of evolution will not continue. Man is not necessarily the end product of evolution. In time our race can expect to evolve into something different, and we can hope that it will be something higher. But the likely alternatives are that man may stabilize in his present form, deteriorate to something lower, or diversify into a number of new forms or species. Or he may follow the giant reptiles and disappear entirely. In the long run, historical odds are strongly in favor of his extinction.

Unlike so many species, however, man has not specialized into a blind alley that can trap him with a minor change in conditions. He is still a relatively generalized construction, adaptable to many circumstances and environments; barring catastrophic changes of environment, man could still modify step by step into other forms to meet new conditions.

At the biological level, man's future is carried in his genes. Were only one couple to survive of all mankind, the race could survive, regardless of how much of its accumulated culture might be lost. Were man to be totally extinguished, even though no other species died with him, it is doubtful whether the continuing forces of evolution would ever cast up another man to walk the world. Circumstances are never twice the same, and had not man's evolutionary development come about as it did when it did, it might never have happened at any other time. Evolution is indeed largely irreversible.

4

Our Crowded Planet

ALTHOUGH we can see the technological path to complete mechanization, there are tremendous social and economic obstacles to its realization. These obstacles are primarily man-made, or, if not man-made, are in the power of man to eliminate, if he chooses to do so.

Thomas Robert Malthus published *An Essay on the Principle of Population, as It Affects the Future Improvement of Society* in 1798, just as the Industrial Revolution was beginning. In essence, he said that because "the passion between the sexes is necessary, and will remain nearly in its present form" and because "food is necessary to the existence of man," a basic dilemma occurs. Because of the passion between the sexes, people multiply, and they do so in geometric ratio, tending to double in numbers every 25 years. The means of subsistence, however, do not and cannot increase at the same rate; at best, they increase in arithmetic ratio, and even this increase depends on bringing new land into cultivation or on making improvements in agricultural methods. Malthus argues that the human population will always increase much more rapidly than the means of subsistence and, therefore, population always tends to rise to the maximum that conditions will permit, being checked only by "moral restraint, vice and misery." The gloomy consequence to be expected from the universal effect of this theorem is that mankind can never be expected to advance above the famine level for more than brief periods of time; as soon as the food supply increases, the population will begin to increase, and this increase, being at a faster rate, will always bring the total amount of food divided by the total population back to the bare subsistence level.

Darwin's theory of natural selection, which derived some of its inspiration from the Malthusian thesis, extended this theory to the plant and animal world. In Darwin's evolutionary world, an unsteady balance exists in nature between the number of each species and the resources available to it. Each species finds its living in the consumption of other species (either animal or vegetable), and most species are in turn food for a larger or stronger species. The relentless struggle of each species to maintain its position in the ecology is popularly called "the survival of the fittest."

Two revolutions began to play a dominant role in the affairs of man soon after Malthus published his book. As a result of these revolutions, the total human population jumped from about 900 million in 1800 to over 3 billion today. The dismal predictions of Malthus did not come to pass. Instead, humanity developed an illusion that the abundant life for all the human race could and would soon be achieved. Malthus was forgotten; it was assumed that the Malthusian law had been repealed.

The first of these revolutions was the Agricultural Revolution, largely a result of opening the vast, fertile, and hitherto untouched American continents to large-scale farming. Much of the rest of the arable land of the world had been farmed for centuries so that it had become steadily less fertile, but the deep topsoil of the Americas had never felt a plow and was ready for the taking. This made available a great and seemingly inexhaustible source of food and fibers to supply all the deficiencies of the rest of the world.

The other revolution was the Industrial Revolution. Tremendous expansion of man's productive powers in the last century and a half not only improved the standard of living but directly increased the food supply available to the world. With improved transportation and communications, more efficient distribution of food followed. New agricultural equipment improved yields from land. Scientific discoveries of new and better foods multiplied the food supply once more.

The increase in the productivity of the farmer and of the industrial laborer brought about a sudden and dramatic outpouring of material goods. Farmers could now feed many more mouths with the same amount of effort, so naturally fewer and fewer farmers were needed and the drift to the city began. Much larger populations per square mile could now be supported.

Back in prehistory before man turned to agriculture for an important part of his sustenance, it is estimated that the world human population was about 10 million. We arrive at this figure because there are about 20 million square miles of fertile hunting land on earth and in a strictly hunting and foraging economy it takes about 2 square miles to support one human. If, for example, more than one family tried to live off the game, berries, and other fruit to be found in a 5 or 6 square-mile area, the food supply would be consumed more rapidly than it could be replenished by natural growth.

When man turned to agriculture, the number of people that could be fed from the same area under cultivation was multiplied a number of times. Until the available farmland became saturated with all the people it could support, there must have been an abundance of food. In such a period, the population would tend to increase rapidly and so long as it could not increase as rapidly as land became available, prosperity would be assured. At its height, for example, the Roman Empire is estimated to have had a population of about 55 million people, yet it covered only a small fraction of the earth's surface.

Whenever new land is opened up or new discoveries permit better use of occupied land, the Malthusian law seems to be inoperative during the period of expansion of the means of subsistence. Despite a lower death rate, the food supply increases more rapidly than the population can grow.

The Industrial Revolution had an additional effect that prolonged the period during which Malthus' theorem did not apply. The new social environment and the new standard of living provided by the industrial economy did not encourage having large families. On the farm it was an advantage to have children to help out with the thousand jobs to be done, but in the city children were an economic liability. The number of children born to the average woman began to decline. In the United States, it dropped in 200 years from eight to three (Brown, 1958, p. 69).

A countereffect also began to operate, but its results were not apparent until recently: medical knowledge, one of the products of the scientific age, began to stretch out the average life-span and thus reduce the death rate. Harrison Brown points out:

When we look back upon the circumstances that led to the growth of industrial civilization in Western Europe, we see, that had conditions been somewhat different, it is possible that the revolution might have been stopped short at any one of a number of points. Of course, a prerequisite was the existence of the necessary major raw materials. But beyond that, it is doubtful that industrial civilization would have arisen had the relation between the number of people and the amount of land not been so favorable, and had the potential increases in food production not been so great. The existence of America and other major colonies, which provided outlets for surplus people and reservoirs of agricultural products, was an extremely important factor. Another factor of importance was medical ignorance. Medical knowledge was increasing steadily, but it was small when compared with that which exists today. Thus, although European populations increased rapidly, the rate of growth was small when compared with rates that would have prevailed had epidemic and endemic diseases been controlled to the extent that is now possible. And finally, people

learned how to limit birth rates. Had this new factor not entered the picture, it is probable that all advances industrialization made possible would have been negated.

*For industrial development to be successful, it is necessary
that production be increased at a rate more rapid than the
rate of population increases.**

Only about one-quarter of the people of the world now
live in countries with so-called industrialized economies,
which are characterized by low birth and death rates and a
very high consumption of material resources per person.
Most of the rest of the world's population exists under conditions in which both birth and death rates are high and
food supply is inadequate for even marginal agrarian societies. Haiti, right on the doorstep of the United States, is a
perfect example. Haiti has almost 5 million people packed
onto half of an island dependent entirely on agriculture.
Haiti's forests have been stripped, and its topsoil is deterio-
rating. Half the population suffers from yaws, an endemic
disease that accompanies conditions of poverty. Haiti is in a
pitiful situation, doomed to recurrent famines, deaths from
which provide the Malthusian check on a very high uncon-
trolled birth rate. The sharp reduction in the incidence of
disease as a result of modern public health measures in
many countries such as Haiti has been no blessing, for starvation must then play the role disease has failed to play
in keeping the number of people in balance with the food
supply.

---

*From *The Challenge of Man's Future* by Harrison Brown. Copyright 1954
by Harrison Brown. Reprinted by permission of the Viking Press, Inc. From
pp. 52–53; italics mine.

In these unindustrialized agrarian economies, the birth rate is so high that no matter how much food we ship to them to augment native supplies, children will be born faster than we can possibly feed them. Even in the industrialized economies, although the rate of increase is much lower, it will be difficult to maintain the present standard of living for an ever larger population.

The combination of a lower death rate and a continued high birth rate is now causing the total world population to increase far faster than ever before. The rate of population increase is approaching 2 percent per year, which, compounded, doubles the number of people every 35 years. Our world now has about 3.4 billion people, so that we can expect 6 to 7 billion by the year 2000 and about 45 billion a mere 100 years later if the present rate of increase continues. Obviously, human population cannot continue to increase at that rate, for we reach an *additio ad absurdum*. Soon there would be standing room only or, at best, a chicken-house or rabbit-warren existence for everyone, even if there is enough food to go around.

How large a population can the world maintain? Even if we consider this a question only in terms of food supply, there is a difference of opinion among the experts. The conservationist William Vogt warns us in *The Road to Survival* (1948) that we have already passed the peak carrying capacity of the world and that a lower standard of living must be expected, even if population begins to level off. His argument is that regardless of future improvements in agricultural methods and more intensive use of available resources, we have already destroyed much of our agricultural capital, the all-important topsoil, which takes thousands of years to form and which can be washed into the ocean in a matter of months when we overcultivate and overgraze the land.

On the other hand, Harrison Brown, in analyzing the potential food sources of the world, sees the possibility of a vastly increased population, provided a tremendous investment is made by man in extracting every possible calorie from the soil and the sea. Algae farms with a yield of 20 tons of food per acre per year could be built in the tropics with a capital investment of about $10,000 per acre. Without such farms, he visualizes a theoretical maximum population of 15 billion; with 1 billion acres of such algae farms, a population of 60 billion could be fed (Brown, 1958, p. 146).

Vogt and Brown do not differ as much as the statements above would indicate; they are working from different premises, but they agree in essence on what must be done. Unless the rate of population increase can be sharply reduced, the economic situation of the world can only deteriorate, for increases in the food supply cannot possibly keep up with an unchecked population increase. Regardless of how many people theoretically could be supported on the earth's surface by the complete and ultimate use of every possible source of food at some time in the distant future, the short-run prognosis is poor.

Vogt is right about man rapidly using up much of his reserve capital of natural resources. Our best soil is being washed into the ocean. We are going deeper and deeper into the earth to supply our mounting demand for the fossil fuels: coal, oil, and natural gas. Our richest metal reserves are rapidly being exhausted, and we are turning to constantly lower-grade ores. Even fresh water, one of the most abundant of all nature's materials, is becoming hard to get in many areas of the world.

Atomic fission was discovered none too soon. We will need atomic energy and solar energy in vast quantities within thirty to fifty years to keep the industrial economies going. If we continue to need vast supplies of metal to support our complex economy, increasingly difficult and expensive extractive techniques will be required.

Industrialization, strangely like evolution, seems also to be an irreversible process. In *The Challenge of Man's Future* (1958), a great book appraising the condition and possible courses of action of mankind, Harrison Brown emphasizes that were the world to revert to an agrarian economy as the result of war or other collapse, it would be impossible for industry to rise again. All the easily available materials have been used up, and industrialism would have to take a single leap to a most advanced stage in order to get at and use the inaccessible materials that are left.

Because industrialized economies have the power to wage completely destructive war, with inadequate controls to prevent it, the most likely prospect is a war that will destroy industrialized society and return the world to a simpler, nonindustrial life bound to the cycle of the soil. Without the support of an industrial complex, such a life would be no idyllic existence; there would be no modern medicine, no machine-made products, none of the amenities that have become second nature to us. A drastically reduced population, living the life of the ancient Eygptian *fellaheen,* would plod wearily behind wooden plows, at the mercy of blind Nature and the elements.

Even if war is avoided, the alternative is the immensely difficult task of changing the present agrarian countries into industrialized nations. Some, like India, are trying to duplicate the past achievements of Japan and Russia in lifting themselves by their bootstraps in little more than a generation. Outside capital is necessary and can come only from the already industrialized countries, for primitive agricultural economies generate almost no surplus for capital savings.

The industrialization of the primitive countries is the only hope to lift the world to a standard of living that will permit free, individual life for all its peoples. If this is not achieved for them, the more advanced economies like the United States cannot expect to live like kings indefinitely in luxury and peace ignoring the hungry rabble outside the palace walls.

But such industrialization becomes possible only if the population growth in these agrarian countries is slowed down or stopped so that adequate food can be provided from the land, not only for the farmers but for those who are taken from the farm to contribute to the building of capital resources. There must be surplus to permit capital formation, and although some of this must be provided at the start from the already industrialized countries (and among these the United States must be a leader), in the long run each country must become able to sustain its own transition to a new kind of life.

There are only two ways to slow up or stop population increase: to increase the death rate or decrease the birth rate. Increasing the death rate can come about only by shortening the span of life. Starvation will remain a factor in determining death rate, despite the triumphs of medicine. The devastation of war must certainly be reckoned as an important influence on population, both past and potential. Atomic warfare could wipe out the entire human race. Conceivably, a higher death rate could be achieved by deliberate slaughter of those deemed by some arbitrary criteria to be excess population, but this alternative, revolting to every sense of humanity, is even less acceptable than the other methods proposed to increase the death rate. Infanticide was practiced by the Greeks and by many other peoples as a eugenic form of population control, but it is not recommended for the modern world.

But the death rate is not likely to increase for any reason short of atomic war. On the contrary, it will probably continue to decrease. In the underdeveloped countries, continued improvements in public health will reduce the effects of disease and tend to lengthen human life to the full span we consider normal in the industrialized countries. At the same time, in the developed countries further medical advances will stretch out that span even more. Medical knowledge and skill will continue to increase so that the lengthening of the life span too, appears to be an irreversible trend.

The only feasible way to stop the population increase, therefore, is to reduce the birth rate, and it is to this means that substantially all the scientific thought in the field has been directed.

Birth control programs on a large scale face some formidable obstacles, however. First, with the present instability in the world political situation, each nation may be inclined to encourage an increase in its own population to improve or maintain its relative political and military strength vis-a-vis its rivals. Second, there are strong religious objections to artificial birth control. Third, because of the abject poverty of those people in the world who need birth control most, any method involving more than the smallest expense is impractical, unless the governments concerned subsidize the program. Fourth, because of the low level of education of so much of the world's population, the practicability of attaining an effective reduction in births by any control that requires the repeated positive action of either or both potential parents is questionable, even if cost considerations are ignored.

In addition to these practical immediate problems, there are three long-term objections more likely to be heard in the years to come. First, there is the economic objection that a free enterprise system thrives only in an expanding economy and that population increase is the best means of keeping it expanding. Second is the objection that the desire to have children as a means of self-fulfillment, which is partly the desire for immortality through one's children, is a strong biological urge. The third objection, discussed in a later chapter, is that stabilizing the world will induce intellectual stagnation with severe long-term consequences.

Whether the efforts of individual countries to stabilize population within their own borders can succeed remains to be seen. Assuming that the religious, economic and social objections can be removed, the political objection remains and cannot be solved by the unilateral action of any single country. Although India, for instance, may at this juncture find it vital to survival to try to halt the swarm of births that is rapidly carrying its overcrowded population of over 500 million to a much higher figure, at some other time a different regime may find political strength in numbers and use an expanding population as an excuse for aggression beyond its own borders in a new cry for Lebensraum. China's present rulers may adopt such a policy of aggression, crammed as that country is with over 700 million people already, even though the government has supported propagation of birth control information.

This desire for fecundity, both at the family and the national level, is not surprising. Nature has created this powerful biological urge for a purpose, and any species that lacks it will soon disappear in the evolutionary race. Among humans, the desire to gain immortality through one's children is natural; custom and tradition consecrate it as laudable. Among proselytizing religions, the best source of new converts is obviously the children of the church members: the more children they have, the more prosperous and influential the church becomes. According to the Roman Catholic position, birth control by artificial means is against God and against nature. The religious argument is a strong one, although its logic is faulty. Although the Church insists that the only acceptable controls are continence or the very dubious rhythm method, it is beginning to recognize the dangers of overpopulation. Many new concepts benefiting mankind have been violently opposed at first as being against God's will—vaccination, for example—until their effectiveness became undeniable. The revolutionary changes in the Roman Catholic Church in the past few years lead one to believe that its position on birth control will change too, and soon.

First, we must ask whether there is any prospect that a substantial reduction in the birth rate could occur without planned programs. In the animal world, Malthusian law does not seem to apply; starvation is the unusual rather than the normal control on population levels. V. C. Wynne-Edwards (1964) points out that most animals other than man maintain their populations at a fairly constant level by other means. This is a complex and little-understood subject, but we are beginning to see that the homeostatic control of population by animal species has evolved as an effective automatic process that inhibits breeding rather than relying on starvation.

> The practice of staking out a territory for nesting and rearing a family is common among many species of birds. In the breeding season each male lays claim to an area of not less than a certain minimum size and keeps out all other males of the species; in this way a group of males will parcel out the available ground as individual territories and put a limit on crowding. It is a perfect example of an artificial mechanism geared to adjusting the density of population to the food resources. Instead of competing directly for the food itself the members compete furiously for pieces of ground, each of which then becomes the exclusive food preserve of its owner. If the standard territory is large enough to feed a family, the entire group is safe from the danger of over-taxing the food supply.*

As Wynne-Edwards further points out, the male that fails to win a territory does not win a mate and therefore does not breed, so that the population level remains constant.

The territorial convention is just one of nature's devices

---

*This quotation and the two following reprinted from 'Population Control in Animals' by V. C. Wynne-Edwards. Copyright © 1964 by Scientific American, Inc. All rights reserved.

to limit and stabilize population; such devices appear in the form of social conventions. Massed maneuvers by flocks of birds occur frequently on clear evenings and are an example of communal activity that appears to have the purpose of providing the flock with an indication of the population numbers. If population density is too high or too low in relation to food supply, the flock automatically increases activities that will improve the balance.

Wynne-Edwards describes how this occurs:

The daily community display puts a changing pressure on the members taking part. If the stress is great enough, a reduction in the population can be triggered off; if it is felt lightly or not at all, there is room for new recruits. Overcrowding will lead to the expulsion of the population surplus, as in the case of the red grouse. In the breeding season the density index, in the form of the daily display, can influence the proportion of adults that mate and breed; likewise the number of young can be restricted in a variety of other ways to the quota that the habitat will allow. (Wynne-Edwards, 1964, p. 72)

Density control in many animals is exercised, he tells us,

by means of a biological reaction—either reduction of the rate of ovulation through a change in the output of hormones, or resorption of the embryos in the uterus as a result of stress (as occurs in rabbits, foxes and deer). (Wynne-Edwards, 1964, p. 74)

Does this have significance for mankind? Although man has no such automatic controls for his population level, we may learn something from them. In one sense, we may say that our present concern about our population problem is a cultural parallel to the instinctual stress controls Wynne-Edwards describes. We may hope that Malthusian starvation need not be the only mechanism to control human population. As Fred Hoyle has said, "there is evidence to show that humans are susceptible to even more subtle feed-back processes than are the birds" (1958, p. 120).

He cites as an example the stabilization of population at a lowered birth rate in England, governed by "the threat of a lowered standard of living." Another example can be found in Ireland, the only country in the world with a de-clining population. The apparent difficulty with this type of population control is that it seems to act as a deterrent to growth only when there is a minimum standard of living, and probably only in a society with a negative view of life. By its terms, it would seem to be ineffective in the abundant economy that we would like to achieve for the whole world.

But the "subtle feed-back processes" are not to be ig-nored. A change in the community attitude toward large families is a subtle feedback, perhaps as effective in the long run as the community displays of the birds. A change in public opinion that would, for instance, permit tax penal-ties for additional children instead of the financial incen-tives now provided by the tax laws could have a significant impact, even without modern artificial methods of birth control.

In the industrialized countries, where levels of education are high, present methods of artificial birth control are effective in keeping family size close to the number planned by each family unit. All the present programs through-out the world are based on encouraging family planning on the assumption that the voluntary choice of each family will slow up and eventually stop population growth. A few decades ago, there was an apparent trend in the United States toward higher-income families having substantially fewer children than those in the lowest income groups. As a result, the hope was expressed that a higher standard of living would automatically act as an adequate brake on population growth. But most families throughout the world still want three, four, or more children, as Kingsley Davis (1967) points out, and therefore complete success of the family planning approach will still leave us with an incredibly rapid population increase. A high enough standard of living will not automatically solve the problem posed by Malthus.

What does limit human population? The food supply is certainly not the only and in some cases not even the major limiting factor. Our recent awakening to the hazards of air and water pollution and to the stresses imposed by excessive noise is an indirect recognition that the practical population limit will not be determined by food supply. When the world becomes crowded enough so that the quality of life falls below the minimum our species is able or willing to endure, population will level off. Air, water, and noise pollution are, in part, a product of our industrial world, but they also tend to increase as a geometric function of the population that that world makes possible. We must recognize that, beyond a certain point, we may be treating symptoms rather than causes when we attack pollution directly.

The spirit and culture of the society has much to do with its birthrate. The peoples of the industrialized countries are no less fecund than those of the agrarian countries, yet the birth rate of the former was much lower long before artificial contraceptive devices were in general use. Special culture traits seem to have an important influence in some cases. In Ireland, for example, the custom of marrying late in life has had an important effect, but we still do not know enough about why Ireland's population has declined. Among the ancient Greeks, the widespread practice of prostitution apparently held down the birth rate and helped keep the Greek population from outrunning its food supply.

Modern organized attempts to control the birth rate have been concentrated in contraception, abortion, and sterilization, in that order. Abortion was an important factor in the successful Japanese program, where the birth rate was cut in half in less than a generation. Legalized abortions in Japan, however, are now being discouraged in favor of better contraceptive control. Today, in the United States, there is a trend toward liberalizing laws that forbid abortion.

Sterilization has had government support in some countries. Two states in India, Madras and Mysore, took the lead in paying subsidies to men who volunteered for the simple, painless operation that renders them infertile (although not impotent). Voluntary sterilization has the advantage of being positive and permanent, but this very advantage is the major objection to it on social and moral grounds.

Principal emphasis on artificial birth control, however, concerns prevention of conception first by mechanical and more recently by chemical means. In the industrialized countries, family limitation by contraception is a powerful force in population dynamics. Even though the application of chemical birth control techniques is still formally forbidden by the Roman Catholic Church, an overwhelming majority of American families, Catholic and Protestant alike, approve some form of family limitation.

Governmental action in many countries has begun and now such action in the underdeveloped nations is receiving support from the United States. In this country the overwhelming pressure of statistics has brought about a remarkable reversal in attitude in just a few years. Harrison Brown stresses that

> Major birth-control programs can rationally be given priority over many aspects of public-health programs, for lowered birth rates automatically result in improved public health. Less frequent exposure to childbearing results in lowered female mortality. Smaller family size results in better nutrition and lowered infant mortality. In addition, the lowered food requirement for an individual family results in generally lowered adult mortality. Thus a major birth-control program can in itself be looked upon as a major public-health program. (Brown, 1958, p. 243)

The world is learning the truth of this analysis.

Research in methods of artificial birth control has been intensive in recent years and continues at an accelerated pace. The most dramatic product of this work to date is "the pill," more technically called steroid-induced pituitary suppression and ovulation inhibition. Although the pill by itself may have a decisive effect on the population of industrialized countries—and there is some evidence that the pill may have had something to do with recent declines in the birth rate in the United States—it is not the answer for the three-quarters of the world in which the problem is the most frightening. Nor will we have time to turn the agrarian economies into industrialized countries. Before that happens, the populations of Africa, Asia, and Latin America will smother us with sheer mass.

The development of technology in the field of birth control, however, may be expected to follow the same ascending curve as all the technology of our civilization. Economic means suitable for the undeveloped world will be discovered and made available within the next few years, if the pace of recent advances is any guide. More and different methods may be expected that will provide positive prevention of conception for extended periods of time at modest cost. Although it is not clear which line of research will be the most successful, the attack is being made in so many directions that it is possible that several different and effective answers will be found.

Let us assume that economical technological means to stabilize world population will be found in the near future. Is this the answer to our problem? If it is assumed that the world population must become stationary in total numbers, how will this be adjusted? Some parts of the world are obviously overcrowded; others are sparsely settled. Some areas are rich in natural resources; others are poorly endowed by nature or have been stripped clean by human greed or necessity. Some nations have higher birth rates than others. How will quotas for birth be allocated among nations and with what terminal result in view? These are colossal problems that defy easy solution.

At the level of the individual, the issue is equally critical. Is each family to be told how many children it may have? Will it be two per family in all cases (perhaps with allowances for inability or unwillingness to have children)? Or will the supposedly superior individuals be expected to have more and the inferior ones none? And who is to decide who is superior and who is inferior, and using what criteria? Financial rewards for "plowing under" one's potential productivity will be effective until we become prosperous enough not to need them. Rewards in the form of prestige for childlessness may become the order of the day; penalties may be exacted from those who find it necessary to continue the family line. What a topsy-turvy world this could be!

Although the drastic efforts of individual countries may be effective in slowing up or even halting for a time the increase in our numbers, birth control will not solve the world population problem for longer than a generation or so unless it is universally applied in accordance with an overall plan. Piecemeal effort will not succeed. The nation or group that practices self-limitation will risk self-extinction if its neighbors do not follow the same rule, for the vacuum will be filled from the high-pressure area. If the intelligent exercise restraint, the unintelligent will inherit the earth. If one nation is successful in maintaining its standard of living by keeping the population in balance with the food supply, its improvident neighbor with the greater population will overflow into its land like a horde of locusts. No Maginot line can prevent this forever.

The right to bear children has seldom appeared on the lists of rights to which man is entitled only because it has rarely occurred to any despot to withhold it; but it is a right as deeply rooted as any and cannot be lightly denied. Yet the rights of the individual and the community must always be held in balance. All our laws are built upon a framework that is a compromise between the interests of both, as each community and generation sees the facts. Population cannot increase indefinitely; at some point, the line must be drawn. Some person or group will have to draw that line and see that it is not crossed.

Sir Charles Galton Darwin considers the prospects for population control in *The Next Million Years* and concludes:

> The fundamental instability of population numbers cannot be checked by man-made laws, and even if it were successfully done for a few years, there is no chance of the system working century after century. (C. G. Darwin, 1952, p. 150)

He pictures world population growing to perhaps three to four times its present number and leveling off only under the pressure of Malthusian law, which he believes will always control human population. In addition to the difficulties already mentioned, he stresses that over long periods of time any artificial system will break down because conditions will constantly change. As an example of a delayed effect, he states, natural selection of humans under these artificial circumstances might strengthen man's present lukewarm procreative instinct (as distinct from his sexual instinct) so much that it defeats the whole program. Darwin is also concerned because if population is artificially limited, natural selection through biological competition would cease to be effective and the race would tend to degenerate.

Taking the long view, he may well be right. We cannot expect any situation to remain static. New forces are likely to arise and set new directions; new attitudes may develop with a different view of life. The very success of world population control will remove it from the top of the list of problems and, in that situation, population may run away again. On the other hand, the same success may lead to a steady decrease in total population that might be difficult to stop short of race suicide. Although the last alternative is far-fetched, we don't know what man may be like in a completely mechanical world.

But these are long-range considerations. In our present crisis, we do not have the luxury of ignoring the immediate problem of sheer numbers of humanity. Nor is it worth giving serious thought to conditions mankind may face a thousand years or more ahead; with our advancing technology, we are changing the face of our world so rapidly that it is foolhardy to guess what we or our environment will be even half that far ahead. The immediate problem must be solved within the lifetime of our young people. The population explosion must be brought to a halt. Slowing up population growth will not be effective; it will only postpone the day of reckoning.

World agreement will be necessary for effective worldwide population control. I do not believe that such agreement can be obtained nor will it endure without the sanctions of some kind of a universal state. The irreversible pressures of technological development that have created the population problem in its modern form will force the world into a single mold by one means or another.

Before considering this possible future universal state and some of the forces that may bring it about, the quality of the future human population must be considered. Population is not merely a matter of numbers; the kinds of people that make it up are vitally important. The basic human type has remained unchanged for at least 50,000 years, but the relentless process of evolution continues.

First, the less adaptable types of man were weeded out. As European man expanded out of his subcontinent a few centuries ago and explored the far corners of the earth, he broke rudely into the isolation of many cultures and racial types. Before his superior military strength, such tribes and nations were largely helpless. European man superimposed a dynamic and complex culture on the lives of simple peoples often unequipped to cope with his concepts. He brought new diseases to which he had become resistant by centuries of exposure; such diseases decimated and in some cases wiped out whole nations. The American Indian, for example, has largely disappeared from our country, except for a few enclaves where he clings to the remnants of a culture hopelessly handicapped in the machine world.

This process will continue. Although there are still many distinct racial types of man, the individuality of these types is maintained in reasonable purity only by physical segregation from other types. In a world that is rapidly growing homogeneous, complete segregation is an obvious anomaly. Western civilization now permeates every corner of the globe. High-speed communication and transportation encourage cultural uniformity and greater mobility among and between peoples. Economic interchange brings social interchange in its wake. An inevitable result is more frequent intermarriage between racial types and gradual blurring of racial distinctions will inevitably follow. Regardless of one's emotional reaction to this prospect, which, among many members of all races is one of distaste, the trend is apparent. We face the prospect that within 200 or 300 years, the species may be as physically homogeneous as its cultural traits are close to becoming today.

A species sometimes evolves into subspecies because of geographical or cultural isolation and the barriers may subsequently be removed or disappear; if the different branches of the species still live in the same general way in the same general environment (in other words, if they occupy the same ecological niche), then eventually only one type will survive.

If, for example, a geological change such as the volcanic upthrust of a mountain barrier divides the members of a species into two isolated groups for a vast period of time, they will tend to diverge from the original species through either change of conditions or nonadaptive variation. If, at a later time, the barrier erodes so that the groups mingle once more, one of three things will happen. If the two groups are not too divergent, they will interbreed and become one species again. If they differ from each other so much that they no longer interbreed, but still lead substantially the same life and compete for the same food in the same way, one group will eventually supersede the other entirely, causing its extinction. If the groups have diverged so much that they now play different and noncompeting roles in the ecology and neither competes directly with any third species, then they may both survive.

As man breaks down the geographical barriers between species by transporting animals and plants around the world and introducing them to lands in which they were strangers, he is inexorably hastening the elimination of countless species that will not survive the intruders' competition. Whether this is good or bad is not clear, but that it is happening is beyond question.

As for man himself, the eventual type that survives, however, may be either the blend of several or all the branches or, alternatively, it may consist only of the progeny of the branch that proves most successful in the intraspecies competition. Because of world-wide cultural intermingling, we may expect a blend of races in this eventual single type, although it is too early to predict which individual characteristics will survive.

Certain evolutionary consequences will follow. Complete homogeneity will end evolutionary development of the human biological organism by means of natural selection. Man will have completed what may be considered an entirely successful biological adaptation to the environment.

Why cannot man continue to evolve as a homogeneous species? The answer is that variations do not tend to take root when all the members of a species are mingled in a single and numerous society. Mutations continue to occur, but because all humanity is joined in a single world group, a mutation that might be favorable in a set of special conditions has no survival value and is lost in the common pool of humanity. Evolution depends upon the ability of those with rare advantageous mutations to establish themselves as distinct from other members of their species, usually in isolated environments with a good deal of inbreeding. Different species develop in different areas from a common ancestor because other mutations appear, some advantageous and some nonadaptive, and come to dominate the entire isolated group because the group is not too large. In addition, the most rapid development occurs when there is room for the greatest number of variations, and this acceleration of evolutionary pace occurs when a new environment is opened up.

When a group is small and isolated, a mutation in a single individual may spread to the whole group in a few generations because of the accidents of survival, whether the mutation is favorable, neutral, or even unfavorable. Variation that accounts for many of the unbelievable number of living species has been quite nonadaptive. Two branches of the same species, living in environments isolated from each other, may have diverged into eventually separate species because the directions taken by the mutations that happened to occur were different in the two groups.

The number of individuals in the evolving group is of first importance. Differentiation occurs only in isolation. A species cannot evolve into two different species when all the members of the species mingle in one interbreeding group. Part of the reason there are over 100,000 distinguishable species of ants is that because of their small size and limited mobility, the world of ants is divided into a vast number of isolated environments in which each community exists generation after generation with no contact with its fellows a mile away.

Evolutionary change, in fact, occurs only in such relatively small isolated groups; a mutation in a single individual, even a substantially advantageous one, tends to be lost in a large interbreeding group.

Natural selection in favor of socially valuable but individually disadvantageous characteristics also occurs only in small groups. J. B. S. Haldane (1966) has shown mathematically that the biological advantages of altruistic conduct only outweigh its disadvantages if a substantial proportion of the group behaves altruistically. If the group is large, the beneficial effect of a mutation in a single individual that increases its altruistic conduct will help the group less than it will hurt the individual, and the individual (and hence the mutation) will not survive. In a small group, the reverse may be true; a mutation that increases the probability of survival of the group, even though detrimental to the chances of the particular individual mutant, may have a favorable survival value.

To some degree evolution is always at work, even in a homogeneous society, but major changes will not come about unless there should be a world-wide change in conditions that persists over a long period of time. For example, if the replacement of oxygen in the atmosphere by the vegetation-carbon cycle failed to keep pace with the loss of free oxygen into outer space so that the percentage of free oxygen in the air declined from the present 21 percent to a smaller figure, all air-breathing creatures would have to evolve larger lungs and larger hearts to continue to have an adequate supply of oxygen. The Indians of the Andes have made this adaptation already, as Darwin pointed out. Those who are born best able to adjust to the thin air have a better chance to survive and thrive. Although the acquired characteristic is not itself heritable, the ability to develop a characteristic can be inherited, and over thousands of years, the blood lines with the capacity to develop larger hearts and lungs have survived better.

But aside from a change in the world environment, the giant strides in man's technical control over his physical environment make unlikely the occurrence of any of the natural circumstances conducive to evolutionary change toward greater selectivity here on earth. Once physical man began to use tools, his biological evolution ceased to be necessary; he could gain complete mastery over nature and adapt to almost all circumstances by using the mechanical forces he was able to harness. With these forces at his fingertips, he needs far less sturdy a body than his primitive ancestors did. On that basis, man is a very satisfactory end product of evolution and, except for minor style changes, needs little improvement.

One major direction in which an improvement of man might be sought is an increase in his brain capacity. Operation of the present brain takes a substantial percentage of man's energy. Were he to need less muscular endowments, however, some of the energy needed for muscular effort could be diverted to feed the requirements of a larger brain. Whether this is a desirable goal is debatable, particularly as man might find it easier to build machines to do the problem solving he might require.

Man can interfere in the biological evolutionary process directly, if he chooses. He has been very successful in improving the qualities of his domesticated animals by selective breeding. Artificial selection of the specimens that are permitted to breed compresses thousands of years of nature's hit-or-miss selection into a few generations. Can man do the same for himself? He may object that it is one thing to improve the size and eating qualities of cattle or the egg-laying abilities of chickens, but quite another matter to improve the character and intelligence of the human race. We have not been breeding cattle for intelligence, however; if we really set about it, we would probably succeed to some degree. The number of genetic variations available today among the human species, many of them recessive, must be immense, and selection among the present stock of genes could vastly enhance the physical and mental strengths of the race as a whole. As Jean Rostand says, "Until human selection has been tried, nobody has the right to assign an upper limit to man" (1959, p. 90).

In going beyond artificial selection and discussing possible mutations in man, Rostand mentions the possibility that mutations may occur (or be stimulated) by increasing the number of sets of chromosomes from two to three or four in man (as has been done artificially in certain animals), which conceivably could result in advantageous characteristics.

In addition to artificial selection and stimulation of certain special mutations (remember that mutations in general are almost always harmful rather than beneficial), individual men may be altered by chemical means. Characteristics acquired in this fashion, however, would not be heritable, so that the race would be improved only if and as long as every member was specifically inoculated. Although tranquilizers are not the first drugs to affect human temperament, they are typical of the crude forerunners of chemicals that may be expected to influence human temperament and intelligence in the future.

In discussing the quality of our future world population, the possibilities of eugenics cannot be overlooked. Certain undesirable qualities in humankind are obvious. The mental defectives, those born with serious congenital disabilities, are not wanted. In recent years, however, we have learned that it is not as easy to make heredity responsible for feeble-mindedness as we believed a couple of generations ago.

Compulsory sterilization of the world's Jukeses and Kallikaks is not the simple answer it then appeared to be. In any case, even if we assign it limited validity, negative eugenics does not scratch the surface of the problem.

A serious problem in regard to man's biological future stems from one of his noblest characteristics, his love of his fellow-man. Our whole concept of the brotherhood of man defies the laws of evolution by refusing to let natural selection do its necessary work. In the nature of things, most mutations are undesirable, and these occur around the world every day. In the animal world, the organism born with a physical or mental defect is less likely to survive in the struggle for existence and thus less likely to reproduce and to perpetuate the faulty mutation. In primitive human society defectives of all kinds were rigorously culled out because, with life perilous and short, only the best equipped survived to the age of reproduction.

But the circumstances of modern human existence have altered the rules. Now every effort is made to prevent natural selection from working at all. Our concept of the brotherhood of man holds that all men are equal, and thus we do everything in our power to insure the survival of every organism that can be called a human being, regardless of his heritable defects. Our humanitarianism permits the survival of many harmful mutations and their bearers are not discouraged from reproducing and thus perpetuating the damaged strains. The life of civilization, contrasted with the sharper struggle of the jungle, shelters the crippled and the stupid. Modern medicine, in stamping out disease everywhere, is making natural resistance to disease unnecessary.

As the environment changes, natural selection becomes positive for changing characteristics. When a characteristic ceases to contribute to viability, selection becomes indifferent to it, so that chance mutations changing this characteristic are not eliminated. For example, certain animals that have adopted a subterranean life for countless generations no longer have the power to see, not because their eyes have atrophied from lack of use but because in the absence of positive selection for good vision, chance mutations impairing vision do not affect the organism adversely and therefore survive. Similarly, if in a workless world or, even sooner, in a welfare state, there is no positive selection for intelligence and physical energy, these qualities will be diminished over the generations.

The individual with a crippling physical disability is not, of course, necessarily unfit to survive. Many great people have been physically handicapped. The potential degeneration in the average level of intelligence is more serious. The range in intellectual capacity among the members of the human race is already greater than in any animal species we know, and this spread between the intelligentsia and the masses will widen as time goes on.

What about a program of positive eugenics to improve the human breed? Defensive eugenic methods such as the sterilization of obvious defectives have received legislative support, although we are far less sure about their validity today than we were a generation ago. But positive methods of promoting the breeding of a superior stock have never received more than cursory attention, despite the obvious parallel with selective breeding of domestic animals.

Our objections to the application of eugenic methods to man are much like those to universal population control. In addition, there are three special obstacles. First, experts cannot agree upon criteria of excellence upon which to base a selection of superior stock. Certain undesirable qualities in humans are obvious, such as mental deficiency; certain types of congenital disabilities might well be culled out. But the determination of what is affirmatively desirable is highly subjective, and until it can be determined which way evolution should go, there is no starting point. How can we judge, without foretelling the future, what kind of a man will be needed in the centuries ahead? Can we do better than nature's shotgun method of storing up a vast variety of mutations within the members of the species in the hope that, no matter how drastically conditions change, some individuals will carry a combination of characteristics that will fit the new and often unexpected situation?

Second, assuming that we can decide what is desirable, how do we breed for it? Our genetic adjustment to our potential environment is so complex that we would be foolhardy to select certain qualities that we would like to strengthen; we could not know, at least given our present knowledge, what collateral effects this choice would have. Even the elimination of an obvious defect might have unforeseen adverse consequences.

A most pertinent example may bring this home. Consider the gene for sickle cell anemia. This recessive gene, when it is passed on by both parents and thus appears in the offspring in double dose (the "homozygous" condition), causes early death from anemia. But when it is passed on by only one parent and appears singly (the "heterozygous" condition), the combination confers unusual resistance to certain serious forms of malaria. In areas of the world where there is a high incidence of malaria, this recessive gene, although fatal in the homozygous form, is advantageous in the heterozygous form. Natural selection has taken into account the respective value of the two factors. It has permitted the incidence of this gene in that proportion of the population (which can be worked out mathematically) which confers the greatest survival value on the breeding group as a whole, even though this means the sacrifice of a certain percentage of children to an early death (Dobzhansky, 1962, pp. 152 ff.).

The case of the gene for sickle cell anemia has several things to say to us. We have an emotional reaction against this apparent need of human sacrifice to permit the group as a whole to survive. Imagine the religious rites that could evolve from the knowledge of how this gene operates; the children dying of sickle cell anemia would be the necessary appeasement of the hungry gods. More calmly, we note that the elimination of malaria by modern public health measures would end the need for natural resistance to malaria and therefore the selective advantage of the sickle cell anemia gene would disappear so that in a matter of generations continued natural selection would substantially reduce the numbers carrying the gene itself. Thus, we would cure sickle cell anemia by eliminating malaria.

The real lesson, however, is one of caution. We learn from this dramatic case the peril of oversimplifying cause and effect relationships, particularly in the extremely complex field of biology. We still know very little, and the more we learn, the more we realize how much more there still is to know.*

In recent years, we have become more aware of our instinctual ties to our animal ancestors. Twenty years ago, we were told that infants were born with only two instincts: fear of loud noises and fear of falling. We were told that these instincts tend to disappear as we mature, so that, as adults, we become entirely products of our environment. Therefore, discontent and aggressive behavior could only be the product of frustration; juvenile delinquency and crime were obviously the products of poverty. Political philosophies have flourished on this faith in the malleability of man; dreams of Utopia have assumed that peace and plenty will automatically satisfy him.

Freud first revealed some of the psychological complexities of our nature. Today evidence is accumulating that man has inherited from his animal ancestors not only his physical structure but many of his cultural traits and behavior patterns. For example, Robert Ardrey tells us that animals seem to have a need for identity, stimulation, and security and that of the three, the need for security seems to come last. He says that many animal species satisfy all three needs by the establishment of mutually exclusive territories by each individual, pair, or group and such territories are vig-

---

*We are learning that equal caution is necessary in dealing with ecologies as a whole. Marston Bates tells us:

A general principle is gradually emerging from ecological study to the effect that the more complex the biological community the more stable [it is]. . . . The intricate checks and balances among the different populations in a forest or sea look inefficient and hampering from the point of view of any particular population, but they insure the stability and continuity of the system as a whole and thus, however indirectly, contribute to the survival of particular populations. (Bates, 1960, p. 261)

85

orously defended when necessary. We are descended, he says, from animals that have a need for aggression for its own sake. In Ardrey's view aggression is not a product of frustration. His analysis of many fascinating studies of animal behavior by scientists of this and the preceding generation on the establishment and defense of territories by individual animals implies that perhaps private property is an instinctual requirement for humankind (Ardrey, 1966).

It is too early to evaluate the effects of these new approaches on human sociology and political philosophy. If, for instance, the institution of private property is an instinctual need of man, what does this say to us about our philosophy of the ideal government and society? And if aggression is not caused by frustration and deprivation but is innate, how does this affect our approach to the elimination of poverty, juvenile delinquency, crime and war itself?

Intimations such as these are one more warning against tampering casually with our genetic nature. We are whole beings, not assemblies of unrelated parts. The winnowing process of natural selection makes its decision against or in favor of the whole animal on the basis of its ability to survive in the total environment, and although one characteristic may make the difference in a particular instance, the line that continues is the one with the best total balance of characteristics that are adequate for the full range of perils it may face. With this in mind, we can be aware how incredibly complex our nature is and accept the statement that with today's knowledge "positive eugenic programs can be defended roughly in proportion to their ineffectiveness" (Lederberg, 1966, p. 519).

Assuming, however, that all these problems could some

day be solved and a sound positive program developed, there is still a third obstacle. How do you obtain the agreement of the participating individuals in any eugenic plan? Imagine the emotional flux in which such a program would flounder. Each of us is convinced that he represents the best and most desirable qualities in human nature, and would find it difficult to accept the assertion that the future of the human race depended on our having no descendants. Passive acceptance of such a veto is bad enough, but positive selection of mates on primarily eugenic grounds would be even more shocking. Geneticists tell us that one answer to this problem is artificial insemination using eugenically superior donors to improve the quality of the race. Few people realize that there are already almost 100,000 children in the United States who were conceived by artificial insemination. The adoption of this technique by so many mothers (with the consent of their husbands) is proof that social and moral problems can be surmounted when the end result is desirable enough.

Meanwhile, natural selection continues, and although a completely pessimistic view is possible, there are positive and beneficial forces at work. Dobzhansky (1967) has pointed out that as caste and class segregation lessen throughout the world and people are freer to select their own occupations, "assortative mating" (mathematician marrying, for example, mathematician) is developing a wider range of abilities in our total gene pool that will give greater variety and therefore greater opportunities in the future.

We sometimes forget that natural selection is influenced by artificial factors set in motion by man in the same way that a change in climate or a development of a new predator may influence which individuals survive and reproduce. Man has had a profound influence on the development and survival of countless species all through his evolutionary history. As a hunter, he decimated countless game animal species and eliminated some entirely. As herdsman and farmer, he cleared out the forests all over the world and thousands of species of animals and plants died out for lack of a home. Other species thrived under the new conditions, developing a symbiotic relationship with man and his way of life. Likewise, man has played the dominant role in determining what are the favorable and unfavorable selection factors for himself, and he will continue to do so.

In the years ahead, our knowledge of ourselves as biological organisms will increase, and this knowledge will help us make the most of our heritage. We will begin to understand the complexities and a few of the many interactions within our own minds and bodies. We are just beginning to realize that the obvious inefficiencies and redundancies of nature provide insurance for survival in catastrophe as well as in normal times and that we must resist the temptation to oversimplify the ecological relationships in seeking to fulfill a short-term goal.

Man does make his own future. In time, he will probably start to consciously remake himself. But this change will not be a major factor in the lives of the few crucial generations just ahead. Long before we change our physical selves significantly we must solve the problem of our total numbers. The necessity to halt the growth of population is inescapable. The choices ahead of us are not easy ones. We know we must insure that man—the unique product of evolution—has a greater, not a lesser future (or none at all). We must protect this future, solving each problem as it arises, acknowledging that we cannot expect to see the path all the way ahead and that, indeed, we can never be sure we are on the main path. We do know that if man does not survive, there is no likelihood that anything resembling him will ever evolve again from the lower levels of life.

If man can avoid total war, if he can stabilize population at a level that permits the good life for all earth's human inhabitants, what then? What will his biological future be? Is it good or bad to have a biologically stabilized and homogeneous species? From the viewpoint of the individual, the world is better off in one big happy family of man. But in the evolutionary sense, the only intelligent being we know has put all his genetic eggs in one basket. Man is closing the door to change in any direction and either he will succeed and survive as he is or he will not survive at all. If past evolutionary history is a reliable guide, this course of action (or, rather, inaction) will almost insure man's eventual extinction, and with his extinction intelligent life will cease on this planet, probably never to reappear.

Were men to be divided into a number of distinct societies so that they were isolated from each other over long periods of time and underwent different environmental stresses, they would evolve either naturally or artificially into a variety of species. In the event of drastic changes in the physical environment, which geological history tells us do appear and will appear again, the likelihood is improved that some group or groups of our distant descendants would be able to survive catastrophe so that the human race would not become extinct.

But we as individuals, like evolution itself, are opportunistic. We are not much interested in remote future contingencies that do not touch our kith and kin, so that this argument seems unreal and unimportant. Yet none of us would like to picture this beautiful earth in years ahead sweeping in its stately orbit around the sun without a soul upon it to exclaim at the beauty of a sunset or to marvel at its myriad wonders.

More immediate, however, is the danger that man will destroy himself, so that insuring his survival even in the near future is a major task for all mankind. Man must take up his problems in the order of their urgency, and that means he must first tackle the ogre of overpopulation and accept the risks of the political world necessary to win this fight. But he must still keep a weather-eye on the enemies over the next hill but one.

5

The Road to Utopia

WHAT are the political problems looming in man's future? Can they be solved by a world state of some kind? The increase in world population combined with the increase in technology (and its child, weapons technology) will probably require a world state in the near future as the only escape from chaos, suicidal war, and the rapid decline of civilization as we know it.

The past history of man shows parallels with the present situation of Western civilization. Two brilliant philosophers of history, Oswald Spengler and Arnold Toynbee, have used these parallels to buttress their arguments that our civilization will develop into an empire and then eventually collapse.

When Spengler wrote *The Decline of the West* just before World War I, he pictured Western civilization bound on the wheel of destiny, fated to pass through the same inevitable cycle on the same inexorable timetable as each of the past cultures he identified as civilizations. At a certain stage in the life of each civilization, a long period of inter-necine struggles and wars is a prelude to the victory of one of the contending states, thus beginning an empire period that carried the civilization through its declining years.

Spengler's faults are obvious. He is extremely dogmatic, particularly when his opinions are most arguable; this irri-tates the critical reader from the start. Nor can one go along with Spengler in his materialistic belief in fate and destiny (a belief for which he owes a considerable intellectual debt to Nietzsche). In treating a civilization that is hundreds of years old as a biological organism, Spengler applies the morphology of life to an inappropriate subject. Finally, in supporting a cyclical view of history, he ignores many facts and reverts to a cosmology that was abandoned centuries ago. Yet, despite these failings, he is a great mystic genius.

Spengler's timetable calls for a universal state over all Western civilization to emerge late this century after a se-ries of increasingly destructive wars. He believes that one country will and must stand out as stronger than the others and, therefore, in Nietzschean terms, superior. So far, 50 odd years later, everything is running on schedule, except that his Germany seems to have been eliminated from the race for power.

When we turn to Toynbee's work, we are in a different world. He divides the species he calls "civilizations" into 21 examples; Spengler recognized only 7 civilizations. Toyn-bee defines Western civilization as the one in which we now live and agrees with Spengler that it arose from the ruins of Greco-Roman (Classical) civilization. Like Spengler, he attempts to show that civilizations follow a cyclical pattern, and because Toynbee is more of a historian and less of a mystic than Spengler, he is more convincing. He finds that these cycles do not follow a definite time schedule and that they vary in pattern depending upon the circumstances each encounters. Above all, his civilizations are not bound on the wheel of destiny; they move from one stage to the next by a natural evolution of circumstances. Toynbee sums up the cause of historical movements in his phrase "Challenge and Response," an explanation very different from Spengler's concept of fatalism.

Toynbee's ostensible goal is to determine by a largely empirical study of the previous 20 civilizations what may be expected of present Western civilization. Only his fellow historians can judge the force and relevance of the evidence he adduces to support the validity of his comparison of civilizations through each of the phases of their respective existences. But whether his argument is valid or not, Toynbee seems to quail at the thought of applying his cyclical laws to the future of our own civilization.

Nevertheless, like Spengler, he sees Western civilization inevitably ending in a universal state or world government and, in order to avoid the prospect of total destruction by atomic warfare, he envisions this coming about by agreement rather than by military conquest. Thus, the cycles of both Spengler and Toynbee lead to the same general conclusion about the future of mankind, although the two men arrive at the conclusion for different reasons.

Will a series of wars or crises force us ultimately into a universal state? This is a paramount question, to which no certain answer can be given. If we believe that history is cyclical in either Spengler's or Toynbee's sense, then it is not hard to follow one or both of them and see the pattern of past civilizations in many of the events of this Western civilization. But eminent historians say that the evidence both use in identifying the alleged similarities of civilizations and cycles is inconclusive and, in fact, the two do not themselves agree how many civilizations there have been, what they were, and what their cycles of growth and decay were.

Even if we were to accept the premise that past history has been marked by cycles of civilization such as Spengler or Toynbee describe, we need not believe that the flow of events will happen in the same way in the future. Their arguments of cause and effect in building a case that the future must follow the pattern of the past are particularly weak.*

Cyclical theories of life have a strange emotional appeal for man. Perhaps we find security in believing that this has all happened before and will happen again and again in the same way. Many religious and mythic cosmologies (Buddhism and the ancient Greek Mythology, for example) embrace cyclical theories of life and history. Perhaps they stem

---

*In justice to Toynbee, however, I quote his recognition that cycles are not the only historical patterns:

Cyclical movements in human history, like the physical revolutions of a cart-wheel, have a way of forwarding, through their own monotonously repetitive circular motion, another movement with a longer rhythm, which, by contrast, can be seen to be a cumulative progress in one direction, even if we cannot be equally sure that this course has ever been set for it deliberately in execution of a plan. (Toynbee, 1956, Vol. IX, p. 296)

from the cycle of day and night, the cycle of the seasons, the cycle of birth and death.[†]

Yet we have learned from science that all these cycles change; that they never occur exactly as before; that life changes, the day and the year gradually get longer; that most apparently eternal cyclical movements are epicycles within greater movements of different kinds, each with a unique pattern to its curve. The pattern of history could just as well be a wave with either ascending or descending nodes or a straight line or the expression of any mathematical equation in functional form.

Under similar circumstances, similar causes are likely to produce similar results. In the long course of history, sets of circumstances at least superficially similar to previous sets of circumstances do arise. Comparisons between modern Western civilization and Greco-Roman civilization are particularly fruitful, and we can compare the "stages" of each civilization with those of the other. The cyclical theory tends to be an oversimplification of these obvious repetitions.

The present world situation is unique in so many respects, however, that it is dangerous to use analogies from previous times, except within the narrow confines of a carefully circumscribed and isolable series of events. Western civilization has now spread over almost the entire globe, at least in its technological aspect, and has absorbed all but a few remnants of all other civilizations. Although the world

---

[†] A recent study suggests that much ancient astronomical learning was derived from an awareness of segments of an even longer cycle, the 26,000 year precession of the equinoxes (de Santillana and von Dechend, 1969).

today is no larger than the Roman Empire was in terms of ease of communication within its boundaries, a difference in sheer size breeds differences in governmental structure. We must be cautious about comparing the actions of 50 million people subject to Roman rule with those of the 3.4 billion people who this earth now numbers as its inhabitants, and who, though they now hold allegiance to many flags, might unite some day in one great polity.

But, although we are politically divided, the world is rapidly becoming one large cultural unity. The fate of mankind lies with this one vast civilization, whatever political form it may take. Ortega once said: "It is sheer madness to stake all Europe on one card, on a single type of man, on one identical situation" (1941, p. 67). Read "all the world" for "all Europe" and the case is even more acute.

Yet we face a dilemma, and here we are approaching the crux of the problem. Although we would rather not stake all on one government, we dare not continue indefinitely in any other way. Universal government of one kind or another, effective to settle the rights of nationalities and individuals, is necessary if for no reason other than to solve the population problem. An adequate world-wide system of population control will eventually have to be enforced by a world-wide authority. Perhaps such an authority need not use force; perhaps it could achieve a stable population by persuasion and education, helped by financial incentives and social pressure, which would temper religious opposition in time. But no matter how it is achieved, population control by some means is the only alternative to eventual mass decimation by war or famine. Until they are controlled, population pressures are bound to bring about explosions of pent-up force that could sweep away much of what we call civilization.

Hanging over all our heads and taking precedence over the other terrors of the future is the power of modern atomic weapons, available at the push of a button to bring about a holocaust that could obliterate man and probably most of earth's other mammals along with him. The awareness that not only could this occur but that it probably would occur if any general war were to start is the most powerful deterrent to the realization of Spengler's gloomy prophecy that the universal empire will be established by conquest.

Can the world state be achieved by peaceful means? The futility of war and the vast benefits to be obtained by cooperation in a common cause should eventually become evident to even the most pig-headed of rulers. But there is no assurance that all will see the light in the same way, that they will be able to implement their judgment, even if they do. Man, after all, is only partly a rational being. Amid present turmoil and tensions, the difficulties of achieving a workless world by peaceful means seem almost insurmountable. So many conflicts of interest and emotion seem insoluble that we despair of working our way through to the end. Defining the problem, however, is a long first step toward solving it.

If, as members of the human race, we begin to understand what the possibilities for the race could be and what basic steps must be taken to make them real, many of the obstacles begin to recede. Furthermore, if we become aware that the goal need not be reached centuries in the future, but be approached within the lives of our children and our children's children, we gain a heightened sense of urgency; we become more willing to subordinate the expediencies of the hour to long-term welfare. Finally, it will spur us to know that the almost certain alternatives to success in this quest are war, chaos, a return to primitive poverty, and possibly complete extinction.

The most frightening of possible futures is the extinction of the human race in a nuclear holocaust. We are all aware of this danger; no one takes it lightly. An attempt to quantify the probability of such an event was made by a group of scientists at a conference on extraterrestrial life at the National Radio Astronomy Laboratory in 1961. In estimating how many "technical civilizations" (that is, those possessing as we do now, the capability of interstellar radio communication) now exist in our galaxy, one needs to know how long the average technical civilization endures before it destroys itself. The scientists' concern about the future of our own civilization is reflected in the selection of two alternate values of L (the life span of a technical civilization) as 10^2 (100) or 10^8 (100 million) years, depending on whether it survives the first and critical period after it acquires the capability of self-destruction. In Sagan's words: "There is a sober possibility that L for Earth will be measured in decades" (Shklovskii and Sagan, 1966, p. 412).

Still another possible future for man could follow anything less than total extinction in a nuclear war. The bitter joke that World War IV will be fought with sticks and stones is an acknowledgment that even if some human life survives a nuclear war, civilization as we know it will be dead. Our machine age exists and grows only because of an extremely complex interrelationship between highly sophisticated entities. It is dependent upon raw materials that today are obtained from deep in the earth or from under the sea by the use of skills and tools that are themselves products of an advanced technology. If, then, much of this fabric of civilization is destroyed, the entire machine technology is likely to collapse with it and man would have to start again at the beginning, but under more serious handicaps than in his first ascent from primitive life.

Despite these dangers, I believe that man will ultimately attain a utopian world. This conviction is not based on blind faith that the story must always have a happy ending. When human attention becomes sufficiently focused on the seriousness of any crisis, things start to happen. As an example very much to the point, only since World War II has the problem of overpopulation been given serious thought by more than a handful of people: yet in that brief time, birth control has changed from a tabooed subject to an important part of the public health programs in a number of countries and in one, Japan, already seems to be outstandingly successful as mentioned earlier. If industrialization can make headway and population can be controlled, the difficulties will begin to fade in years to come. These programs will bolster each other; the less people in the world, the larger the individual share will be.

The political "how?" remains unanswered. Will it be achieved by peaceful agreement or by conquest? Will the universal world state be a dictatorship, a form of democracy, a confederation of equals, or a new entity that we do not anticipate? We can only wonder. The world political balance, complex and unstable, is itself subject to the forces of acceleration evident in all our economies; what is true

99

today is no longer true tomorrow. History has no certain outcome, and the means it uses are often obscure and accidental. We can estimate the long-range probabilities from the facts and figures at our disposal, but although we can predict with some assurance approximately how many times in 1,000 tries a coin will come up heads, we have no answer on which way the next toss will fall.

If man as a species can master his own nature sufficiently to cooperate with his fellows on this global scale, he has it in his power to provide for all the race a long, prosperous, and peaceful life; to maintain this idyllic state the individual would expend only the amount of effort he feels moved to exert. Throughout his prehistory and history man has searched for this supernal world either in heaven or on earth.

Will he be satisfied? Should he be satisfied? So certain am I that this universal state is man's probable future here on earth that thus far this book has been only a platform from which these two questions—so crucial to man and perhaps to the whole universe—can be asked.

6

The Torpid Society

IS a peaceful leisure state an adequate final goal for man? And if it is achieved, can restless man endure it? To answer these questions, we must consider man's place in nature. We must be aware of what he can and cannot do about the world around him, and although recognizing the qualities and abilities that set him apart from his animal forebears, we must be aware of the parts of his nature that derive from them. The answers to both questions are negative, as this chapter will argue, and thus the human predicament will confront us face to face.

In our study of life and the universe, we are bound to take the anthropocentric view. Even though man is now aware that this planet is satellite to a small star on the outer edge of a vast galaxy which is itself only one among more than a thousand million galaxies, he is not overawed by its vastness compared with his own puny strength. As a surveyor starts from a known bench mark, so must man start from himself and look outward.

Chance events do determine much of the course we are to follow. Single men, at the forks of history, themselves insignificant and unperceiving, have cast the die that changes the course of the world because they happened to be at the right place at the right time. A single mutation in a microscopic gene may set off a new evolutionary direction. Conception itself, the fortuitous meeting of one out of a vast number of sperm with the receptive female cell, determines whether we have a Leonardo or a nonentity.

The human race as a whole, and all of us as individuals, have times and occasions when we are swept helplessly on the tide of events, and little we do has much effect. But these are followed by other times when the puny force we command becomes decisive in setting the course. We feel we have, and we do have some control over events; we do not have to agree with Leo Tolstoy that just because we do not recognize all the effects of our acts, we are mere flotsam on the river of destiny.

By nature, man is unwilling to consider himself insignificant. The will to live is part of the biological heritage of all living creatures. Nature has endowed us with a substantial dose of this powerful medicine. Even though life seems hopeless to many people, suicide is rare; this is not accidental. Nor is it a coincidence that the stagnant quietism characteristic of Hinduism, the goal of Nirvana, or nonexistence, arose in a torpid society in which the mass of the people were enduring grinding poverty. In view of today's surge of interest in certain aspects of Buddhism and Hinduism, Will

Durant's comment many years ago, in summing up his analysis of these philosophic systems, has particular point.

> . . . there is a depth in these meditations which by comparison casts an air of superficiality upon the activist philosophies generated in more invigorating zones. Perhaps our Western systems, so confident that "knowledge is power," are the voices of our lusty youth exaggerating human ability and tenure. As our energies tire in the daily struggle against impartial Nature and hostile time, we look with more tolerance upon Oriental philosophies of surrender and peace. Hence the influence of Indian thought upon other cultures has been greatest in the days of their weakening or decay. (Durant, 1935, p. 553)

Man is biologically a hunter: he is carnivorous, not herbivorous. When man's distant ancestors came down from the trees, they learned to hunt. During all but a few thousand years of his existence on earth he has been a hunter, finding his prey where he could and living from it. This is part of his instinctive heritage.

Besides being a curious animal, man is also restless, his restlessness has been a biological advantage in building a new way of life.

> Men seek rest in a struggle against difficulties; and when they have conquered these, rest becomes insufferable. . . . it is the chase, not the quarry, which they seek. (Pascal, 1941, pp. 50–51)

As restless creatures, we are not long satisfied with any achievement; we share a compulsion to take one step further, and still another. Not all civilizations may have the dynamic drive of our own Western civilization, but although there is plentiful evidence that, by our standards, many human societies are lazy, shiftless, and torpid, I believe that all have latent vitality.

Peaceful rest is not man's goal. Only in the mind of a Hamlet does "that sleep of death" find attraction. This urge to grow is not new. In eleventh-century France, cathedral building was a mass expression of a desire for something greater, which Henry Adams called "an emotion, the deepest man ever felt—the struggle of his own littleness to grasp the infinite" (1925, p. 106). Aspirations for the infinite are more conscious today. Man is reaching out; he needs to breach old frontiers and blaze new trails both physically and intellectually.

Man is forever seeking that will-o'-the-wisp, happiness, even though he does not know what it is. His desire for self-expression spills out in his work, in his art, in everything he does; it cannot be denied. The best reason for setting about the dangerous and difficult ascent of an unconquered peak still is "because it is there."

Assuming all this, suppose we find that an earthly utopia is almost within our grasp, a peaceful universal state benignly supervising a substantially workless world. Is this bucolic existence to be the ultimate goal of humanity? When we have succeeded in making man superfluous on earth, do we go on living happily ever after? Will we be content in this death in life? I do not believe that a negative philosophy of life will succeed in a dynamic society, nor will a positive philosophy endure in a static society.

Goals, however, are still set forth in largely static terms.

In the Middle Ages it was appropriate to describe heaven as a place of rest. When men were overworked and underfed, peace was the only ultimate that could be expected to have appeal. Yet almost every philosophic utopia has been equally soporific. Plato's *Republic* called for a vigorous life, an aristocracy of the educated, it is true, but with no change in the nature of the state from generation to generation, with no concept of improvement except by refinement; the stage remains the same, only the players change. We should expect this of Hellenic society, which was static in concept as contrasted with the dynamic Western civilization.

The word "utopia" designates an ideal human society; it was derived by Sir Thomas More from two Greek words meaning "nowhere" and was used in his book *Utopia* published in 1516. More's Utopia is a tightly controlled, and static society that functioned effectively even by its own terms only because it was inhabited by a remarkably tractable people. The leaders provided paternalistic, although benevolent, supervision over the affairs of the state. But whatever the people of More's time thought about the way of life described, today most of us would see it as dull fare indeed and opt for more variety of atmosphere and some possibility of change.

More's *Utopia* like Plato's *Republic,* on which it was partly modeled, requires bondsmen or slaves to keep the economic wheels turning. More was also aware of the problems of population growth and his utopia provided for a carefully controlled emigration to new and uninhabited lands elsewhere as its outlet for surplus population.

In our sophisticated and restless times, we may look at this utopia and laugh a little but, in the setting of the early sixteenth century it was a remarkable vision. It was far more than a century later before anyone had a conception of history as a process, not merely a recital of the genealogy of monarchs. Human nature was assumed and believed to have been invariable since the Creation. It was not possible for medieval man to conceive of anything but a static society. Only a few were just beginning to wonder if there could be rewards on earth such as most men assumed could be found only in heaven.

Then the ferment of the Renaissance began. J. B. Bury later described the change this way: "The hope of an ultimate happy state on this planet to be enjoyed by future generations . . . has replaced, as a social power, the hope of felicity in another world" (Becker, 1949, pp. 7).

Yet with all that the human race has learned since that time, our visions of utopia have improved only in details: we still dream of a static society. We delude ourselves that a static heaven will contain a restless, headstrong, and often irrational species. Every ideal society from Plato's republic of over 2,000 years ago to the many attempts by communist and socialist idealists of the last century to create a true utopia on earth has ignored the wild and contradictory nature of man.

In *Looking Backward* (1951), Edward Bellamy portrays an idealized future communistic utopia in conservative Boston, bucolic and static, frozen at a technological level far below what has been achieved already. In *Men Like Gods* (1923), H. G. Wells spelled out what might be expected in his ideal society, a planet limited to a population of 250 million people, all physically beautiful and highly intelligent from centuries of eugenic breeding. His middle-class hero from earth finds these brilliant intellectuals working on advanced scientific projects in a dedicated but unhurried way. Their uniform beauty leaves no room for individuality or the kind of genius that in the past has been the product of abnormality. These utopians are the archetype of W. D. Whyte, Jr.'s Organization Man. Only the gray flannel suit is missing. They are a cold people, and Wells is unable to inject the spark of life into them.

As we approach the possibility of realizing these dreams, it becomes more apparent that they leave much to be desired. No one has pictured the problem better than Aldous Huxley in *Brave New World* (1932), a novel written forty years ago. It is a must on the reading list of anyone concerned with the future. Here is the ultimate static society: its rulers insure by constant administration of a euphorian anesthetic that ignorance remains bliss. All values disappear, for nothing can be important; the world is a playground for mental ten-year-olds who never grow up. In *Nineteen Eighty-Four* (1963), George Orwell portrays a world dictatorship in which everyone but the rulers live in the equivalent of a glass-walled zoo. A generation earlier, H. G. Wells, in *The Time Machine* (1931), looked far down the corridors of time and showed future mankind reverting almost to the level of the rabbit.

Modern science fiction is packed with such estimates of the future. Although most show little imagination, a few are outstanding. In *The City and the Stars* (1956), Arthur C. Clarke, one of today's leading writers of science fiction, pictures Diaspar, a highly advanced civilization of the far-distant future. Its citizens are freed from all work by complete mechanization, and they have virtually eternal youthful life on earth and can command every conceivable pleasure and excitement merely by asking for it. Diaspar is a completely happy but static state in which people are conditioned to accept the way things are and to leave unquestioned the possibility that there is anything beyond. In the supposedly contrasting civilization of Lys, Clarke described a free people who, though enjoying the comforts of a highly mechanized society, prefer a simpler, rural life. Having had the choice between mortality and immortality, they deliberately chose the former to give life direction and meaning. But Lys, too, is static, largely because it has developed as far as we in our times have the imagination to envision, and we can think of nothing more to add.

There cannot be a perfectly happy society. Perfection implies completion, and man cannot be happy or fulfilled in a completed society. One writer puts the problem thus:

> Happiness does not come from a state, but from a change of state. That it is so is illustrated by the total failure of every writer to describe a satisfactory paradise, whether in heaven or on earth. The tedium of eternity has almost become a joke, and the description of the earthly utopias are no better. Most of them fail to recognize that the human mind cannot hold any emotion for long at an even intensity, but that it always degenerates into something much more tepid. . . . But it is not simply a change of state that makes for happiness; there must be something unexpected about it. (C. G. Darwin, 1952, p. 159)

Goals must be beyond reach in order to serve their purpose. Clarke touches on this dilemma when he writes, "there is a special sadness in achievement in the knowledge that a long-desired goal has been attained at last, and that life must now be shaped toward new ends" (1956, p. 305).

C. P. Snow puts the matter even more sharply in describing how a scientist, immediately following an important triumph "was sick with that depression, that sense of clear-sighted futility, which comes to us all with the achievement of what we have greatly desired" (1934, p. 206). If mankind is to be true to itself, it needs ever new goals, new challenges, and new difficulties. If it is to live instead of sleep, our species will always need new and more difficult problems to solve.

But the prospect here on earth is dismal indeed. Huxley's *Brave New World* may be a blueprint of the future. Roderick Seidenberg has spelled out the darkest picture of the future in his closely reasoned *Post-historic Man*. His argument is that man, aided by the machine, is developing a steadily greater dominance of intelligence over instinct and that through the growth of all kinds of organizations

> intelligence, which today is looked upon as the gift of the individual, may in time be accepted instead as an ingrained attribute of society as a whole, displacing our common impulses by an equally common rationality (Seidenberg, 1950, p. 178).

Consciousness, Seidenberg believes, is an imbalance between instinct and intelligence, and therefore the kind of change we call "history" occurs only when those forces work against each other to create a precarious equilibrium in man. According to his thesis, society will eventually be so completely organized by intelligence that it will become static and man will be encased in an endless routine and sequence of events, not unlike that of the ants, the bees and the termites. . . . Thus we are led to perceive that history itself, however inclusive we may conceive its sway, must be counted in reality as a high transitional area of relatively short duration in comparison with the slumbering eternity that preceded it, or the ever more static ages that will follow upon it. (Seidenberg, 1950, pp. 179–180)

The survival of individuality depends upon the success of the creative minority in avoiding being smothered by and absorbed into the uncreative mass that moves relentlessly away from individuality toward conformity and collectivism. Seidenberg quotes from Toynbee the following significant paragraphs:

In every growing civilization, even at the times when it is growing the most lustily, the great majority of the participant individuals are in the same stagnant quiescent condition as the members of a primitive society which is in a state of rest. More than that, the great majority of the participants in any civilization in any phase are men of like passions—of identical human nature—with Primitive Mankind.

. . . There is an overwhelming majority of ordinary people in the membership of even the most advanced and progressive civilization; and the humanity of all these people is virtually primitive humanity. (Toynbee, 1955, Vol. III, p. 243 quoted in Seidenberg, 1950, p. 223)

Carl Becker says the same thing with a different emphasis:

The mass intelligence functions most effectively at the level of primitive fears and tabus. . . . The exceptional few have little in common with the undistinguished many, except the implements of power and the symbols of wealth with which to obtain them. (Becker, 1949, p. 107)

Later, he says:

The forces of Nature have been discovered and applied by a few exceptional individuals, whereas every effort to ameliorate human relations has been frustrated by the fact that society cannot be transformed without the complacence of the untutored masses. (Becker, 1959, p. 104)

Man is the same creature biologically that he was 50,000 years ago, with the same inherited intelligence. Although we may be able to modify man for the better biologically in distant generations, at present the changes will have to be brought about by education—what Toynbee calls "mimesis." If civilization is to advance and not to freeze organizationally at the lowest common denominator of intelligence, there is no time to waste. H. G. Wells summed up the situation in a phrase: "the race between education and catastrophe."

The pressure of our growing population accentuates the trend toward more complete and world-wide organization. The influence of a dense population is implicit in Seidenberg's argument that the complete victory of intelligence over instinct will bring man's history to an end and turn it into an ageless post-history to continue forever like a world-wide ant hill. The closer we are packed together, the more we must adjust and conform to the mass criteria in order to survive and the more rapidly the will of the mass will suppress the individual spirit. We see this trend everywhere. The cult of conformity is symptomatic of the trend and, it, in turn is fostered by those who believe in a kind of "progressive" education that stresses the need for training for "life adjustment" to the "peer group" rather than in knowledge as strength to free oneself from reliance on mob opinion. The individual is being absorbed into the group, the company, the club, and the gang.

The prospect of a static state is not a chimera; it is very real and near. In a letter to Toynbee, the historian Edwyn Bevan voiced his fear thus:

> I do not think the danger before us is anarchy, but despotism, the loss of spiritual freedom, the totalitarian state, perhaps a universal world totalitarian state. . . . As an alternative to anarchy, the World would welcome the despotic state. Then the World might enter upon a period of spiritual "petrification," a terrible order which for the higher activities of the human spirit would be death. (Do you know Macaulay's essay on "History"? He argues that the barbarian invasions were a blessing in the long run because they broke up the petrification. "It cost Europe a thousand years of barbarism to escape the fate of China." There would be no barbarian races to break up a future world totalitarian state.) (1955, p. 9)

Barring atomic extinction, the pressures of the world's economies and the tidal wave of human fertility will force man into a world-wide universal state. Such a state will eliminate, or at least submerge, most of the tension and pressures of political life. The need for vast military arsenals will cease, freeing a large part of the world's energies for peaceful projects.

If man so permits, the continuing advance in technology will create machines that can do all the work of the world and eventually all its thinking too. And man could easily become an appendage to such a smoothly functioning, complex economy. In a world state, a completely homogeneous society would provide little encouragement for creativity and originality; on the contrary, it would place a premium on conformity and mediocrity. In such a torpid world, man would be quite willing to let machines take over; he would fail to recognize that he might be signing his own death warrant as a species, when the machine "species" begins to fill his ecological niche.

How would a machine takeover actually come about? With our present understanding of evolutionary forces, we can write a tentative script of what the sequence of events might be.

Assume that we arrive at a universal world state with a stable population. Assume that technology on earth continues to expand, even if at a level or declining rate, so that machines perform a growing proportion of the tasks of civilization, first physical and then mental. In the torpid society, man will become steadily more dependent on machines to carry on the functions of the society. As these machines begin to supply all man's needs, including not only subsistence but also administration and planning, the machines will become interconnected in a system that is self-reproducing and self-perpetuating. In time, people will cease to know how to build, maintain, or repair the machines. Eventually they will not even bother to know how to run them.

The machines and their entire system will be designed to serve the needs and desires of man. They are not Frankenstein monsters but are quiet, unobtrusive and man-centered. But, in a real sense, the laws of evolution will apply equally to inorganic matter as to organic functions, although in a different way. As machines wear out and are replaced, changes in design will occur from time to time, roughly parallel to mutations in organic beings. Mistakes are made even by machines because they are as much subject to the rules of probability as the templates we call genes that determine human construction.

So long as man exercises control, if changes in the machine system detrimental to man occur, he will see that they are reversed. Long after man ceases to control the machines himself, the machines will still be programmed to avoid hurting mankind. But just as natural selection is neutral to the quality of eyesight of animal species that live permanently in a subterranean environment, so will the evolution of machines be neutral to man's welfare when his influence on the operations of the machine world ceases.

Eventually, therefore, selection will cease to work in favor of changes that improve man's condition; instead, selection will become indifferent to man's welfare. Therefore, changes that may inadvertently damage man or work against his best interests will have as much survival value as those that do not. Such damaging changes, singly or cumulatively, will eventually be fatal to man unless he is able to regain control in time. But once man's control is lost, and with it his drive for creativity and leadership, reversal will be impossible.*

In *Aku-Aku* (1958), Thor Heyerdahl gives a clear example of the decay of creativity in a frontierless society on Easter Island. His excavations and experiments support the conclusion that Easter Island was populated centuries ago by adventurers from the rich Incan civilization, whose descendants lost contact with the mainland. In this circumscribed world, the sculptural expressions of the Incan cultural heritage produced by each generation gradually degenerated into gigantic stereotypes, and then, after many generations, not even stereotypes were made. Creativity gradually died as the society drifted into a vegetative existence.

This state of affairs may seem remote to us now, and at the moment, we would gladly trade the tensions and troubles of today for a more peaceful world; but it would be an exchange we would later regret. Events are marching rapidly and almost relentlessly toward its realization in the universal world state in the relatively near future. We may obliterate ourselves in war, perhaps, but, on the other hand, we may reach utopia on earth in a handful of years.

If we are to continue to realize the potential of the human race, new goals will be necessary, and there is only one place that these goals can be found. Now that every corner of our globe has been explored, new frontiers are needed. The only possible new frontiers are those outside our world—in space.

---

*Years ago E. M. Forster wrote "The Machine Stops," a short story that relates what could happen when we lose control over our child, the machine (1928, pp. 13-85).

7

On Other Worlds

MAN is now opening the door to the most expansive and exciting period in his history. It began when Sputnik I, the first Russian satellite vehicle, swept into free orbit around the earth in October 1957. We sometimes call our present times the Atomic Age. If part of the recent past is to be marked off as the Age of Steam and the Age of Electricity, then it is appropriate to call the period that began a quarter of a century ago under the Stagg Field grandstand at the University of Chicago the Atomic Age. If man's progress is measured in terms of physical power, atomic power is a proper sequel to steam and electric power. The release of the energy to be obtained from intra-atomic change would seem to be the ultimate power source available to us—a genie, in fact, able to perform any miracle we can dream of.

Yet, although atomic power is in its infancy, with its giant potential scarcely tapped, its ultimate importance to mankind is already overshadowed by new possibilities arising from the sudden advent of the Space Age. No matter how much we change the face of the earth with the use of atomic power, it will have far less effect on our future than the stark fact that man is beginning to reach out into space. We cannot but be awed by the thought of stepping from the surface of this beautiful world into the dark emptiness that surrounds us. This is a different kind of change than was begun at Kittyhawk in 1903. The airplane is a mere extension of our life on the ground, and, like Antaeus, it returns frequently to the ground to replenish its strength. But the long adventure cannot always be made with one foot on home base. The distances are so vast that once the bold plunge is made, many of the journeys will be only one way: out.

The exploration of space is as great an adventure as that of the first creatures to come out of the sea a billion or more years ago to live on dry land. This, perhaps the greatest previous adventure in the history of life, was achieved slowly and painfully, by a thousand gradual changes, and then only by our ancestors bringing much of the sea world with them in their bodies. Man's time to adapt to new possibilities will be far less, and the changes involved may be far more severe.

The possibilities of space exploration have come upon us suddenly. Writers of science fiction have been spinning lurid tales about the worlds above for almost a century, but little attention has been paid to their fantastic stories. And because the stories have been compounded from a very small dose of fact and a preponderance of dream, some of them have received less attention than they deserved. This is not, however, to their discredit. There has been little or no data to go on. We know so little about the universe and much of what we do know has been learned in this generation. Little wonder that there has been such wild speculation.

Now, all of a sudden, the power to cross this frontier is within our grasp, and imagination runs riot because of all the opportunities that have been revealed. The sky is no longer the limit; there is no limit that we can mark to what may be tried. Space is infinite, or if it is not (and we do not know yet), it is closer to infinite than man can possibly imagine.

Do we really want to go out into space? Aldous Huxley strikes a conservative note in a recent book:

> . . . all our exuberant post-Sputnik talk is irrelevant and even nonsensical. So far as the masses of mankind are concerned, the coming time will not be the Space Age; it will be the Age of Over-Population. . . . And even if, at some future date, emigration to Mars should become feasible, even if any considerable number of men and women were desperate enough to choose a new life under conditions comparable to those prevailing on a mountain twice as high as Mount Everest, what difference would that make? In the course of the last four centuries quite a number of people sailed from the Old World to the New. But neither their departure nor the returning flow of food and raw materials could solve the problems of the Old World. Similarly the shipping of a few surplus humans to Mars (at a cost, for transportation and development, of seven million dollars a head) will do nothing to solve the problem of mounting population pressures on our own planet. Unsolved, that problem will render insoluble all our other problems. Worse still, it will create conditions in which individual

freedom and the social decencies of the democratic way of life will become impossible, almost unthinkable.*

Huxley is indisputably right; sending a few people to another world will solve no problems here. Colonization is not the answer to the population problem. Planetary colonization will not have a direct effect on the great majority of us, who will remain on our own soil.

But that is not the point. There is no evidence that anything out in space will solve today's problems here. What, then, is the role of a transtellar civilization in influencing life on earth? The answer, it seems to me, is that it will introduce fresh ideas and new forces into our earthly society in time to stave off the torpor of a static universal state. It will awaken mankind on earth to new vistas and new purposes.

I do not ignore or underestimate the pressing problems we face on earth. The fish in the sea still had the same overpopulation problems after the first creatures had crawled up on land. The conquest of the new world above the water level never alleviated any problems in the sea. It is possible that future adventures in space may have adverse effects for man on earth, just as man and his technology have probably worsened conditions for the denizens of the deep that never emerged. That is the risk we must take.

It is none too soon to begin serious study of the potential implications of life on other worlds, not just in regard to technical difficulties but to our whole philosophy of life and to man's place in the universe. These are among the most serious questions man has ever asked.

*From Aldous Huxley, *Brave New World Revisited* (New York: Harper & Row Publishers, Inc., 1958) p. 11, by permission of the publishers.

Many of these questions have already been raised in the pages of science fiction. Forget the crude stories about tentacled villains from Mars who battle our hero along the spaceways; there is an incredible amount of trash that calls itself "science fiction." I refer instead to tales in the tradition of Mark Twain's *Connecticut Yankee in King Arthur's Court* and Jonathan Swift's *Gulliver's Travels,* which use strange and unreal confrontations as a milieu in which to pose social and philosophic problems in their most biting form.

Science fiction is not just for children. On the contrary, the forward thinkers in that field should engage the attention of all of us. The rapid success of science fiction during the present generation is a recognition of the need for new frontiers and a realization of where they are.

With the growing sophistication of the reading public, the writer of science fiction has an increasingly difficult time making his stories seem credible without becoming so entangled in technical language that the main theme is lost. But he can place human problems in new perspective in order to sharpen our focus on the problems ahead. Huxley's *Brave New World* is the classic and frightening example. Disguised as science fiction, H. G. Wells' *The Time Machine* is one of the earliest and most perceptive speculations on the future of mankind. Only if we speculate on possible futures can we begin to define desirable goals.

Arthur C. Clarke has put the matter bluntly:

that the world is now space conscious, to an extent which would have seemed unbelievable only a few years ago, is a statement that needs no proof. But it is not yet space *minded*. By this, I mean that the general public still thinks of space activities almost exclusively in terms of military strength and international prestige. These matters are, of course, vitally important; yet in the long run, if there is a long run, they will be merely the ephemeral concerns of our neurotic age. In the sane society which we have to build if we are to survive, we must not forget spacemanship and concentrate on space. Unfortunately, altogether too many educators, intellectuals and other molders of public opinion, still regard space as a terrifying vacuum, instead of a frontier with infinite possibilities.*

For a civilization that from its beginning has been characterized by its dynamic energy and its groping for the infinite, it is appropriate that at this time the vast expanse of the heavens should open up above it. Perhaps we have seen only the first inkling of man's future greatness.

In these times, hardly a week passes without some new happening that the daily press describes as concerned with space. What is "space"? In popular terminology, it means everything in the entire universe in all directions outside and above the earth's atmosphere. It is immense beyond all imagination, and yet we may know only the smallest fraction of it. In fact, if it is infinite, the part we can see to the limit of the range of the 200-inch Palomar telescope is not that smallest fraction, for infinity cannot be fractionated.

The scope of astronomical knowledge has expanded at an accelerating pace in the past few years, perhaps more than any other science. New tools for studying the skies

---

*From Arthur C. Clarke, *Voices From The Sky*. (New York: Harper & Row Publishers, Inc., 1965), p. 12, by permission of the publishers.

have made this possible, and in astronomy particularly, the benefits of the feedback of mechanical technology on basic scientific research are tremendous. The 200-inch Palomar telescope, which took years to build, has rewarded us with its ability to see much farther into space. The new field of radio astronomy has opened an important window on the sky. New cameras and films, new optical techniques, and new recording and computing devices all have contributed to a better view of the heavens and a better understanding of what is seen.

Constant and intensive studies by a large number of dedicated scientists, not only in astronomy, but in chemistry, physics, geology, and other fields have thrown light on many problems; answered some questions; and raised new ones, many still to be answered. Many major concepts of astronomical theory have been uprooted in this last generation, and more will doubtless require critical review as new information comes in. Yet many statements can be made with as much certainty as we can have about anything outside our own world.

In any discussion of astronomy, it is appropriate to start with our own earth in our own solar system. This slightly pear-shaped sphere, about 8,000 miles in diameter, is one of eight planets traveling in a nearly circular orbit around the sun and which are all in almost the same plane. (Recent studies indicate that Pluto, the supposed ninth planet, is in a very eccentric orbit and may not be a true planet after all.) This sun has a diameter of about 865,000 miles and is, on the average, about 93 million miles away.

The vast empty distances of astronomy are little more than unreal figures to us. It is helpful to bring the scale down to a size within our daily experience, if we are to comprehend at all. Assume that the 8,000-mile diameter earth is just 1 inch in diameter, or about the size of a Ping-Pong ball. On that scale, the moon will be about 30 inches away and about ¼ inch in diameter. On the same scale, the sun will be 970 feet (or about 1/5 of a mile) from the earth, and will be 9 feet in diameter. Seven other planets besides the 1-inch earth circle around this 9-foot sun. Mercury, ½ inch and Venus, 1 inch in diameter, are between the earth and the sun. Half again as far away from the sun as the earth is Mars, slightly more than ½ inch in diameter. Beyond it are Jupiter, a semisolid 11 inches; Saturn, 9 inches; and Uranus and Neptune, 4 inches each. Neptune, the farthest of these, is about 5.5 miles from the sun. Many of the planets have one or more moons, ranging in size from the 5-mile diameter Diemos circling Mars, which would be a grain of sand on our scale, up to Titan, which is larger than Mercury, circling Saturn.

Except for the sun, these planets, and their few moons, there is nothing else in this entire space except some asteroids and meteors, the largest of which would be specks of dust on our 1-inch scale. With the exception of the 9-foot sun, every planet, moon, asteroid, and meteor in the entire solar system, a space with the sun as its center and a diameter of over 10 miles could be swept up and packed into a large suitcase. How empty space is!

If we look for other habitable worlds in the solar system, we see little promise of potential success. The outer planets from Jupiter to Neptune can be canceled out at the start because they are too cold for man (-200° F. or colder), even if they were not uninhabitable for other reasons. Turning to the inner planets, we have long since eliminated Mercury as being too hot (up to 750° F.). This leaves only Mars and Venus.

In the last few years, we have learned much more about Venus. In October 1967, both a Russian and an American unmanned spacecraft entered the Venusian atmosphere. The Soviet craft parachuted a landing capsule that transmitted a variety of information until it landed. The U. S. craft conducted a number of scientific experiments as it swept past and on out into solar orbit. In May 1969, two more Russian spacecraft parachuted instrumented capsules into the atmosphere. As a result, previous evidence that the temperature of Venus was 500° F. or higher has been confirmed, so we know that life as we understand it cannot survive there, at least on the surface. In addition, the capsules recorded atmospheric pressures of 27 earth atmospheres even at an altitude of many miles so that pressures at the surface must be from 60 to over 100 times the pressures on earth. Our dreams of Venusian charms have faded.

Even more is known about Mars. Although it is one-half the diameter of the earth and only one-tenth of its mass, it is more like the earth than any other planet. But it is scarcely a habitable world. It has an exceedingly thin atmosphere, far less than at the top of Mount Everest; it has an approximate 24-hour day; its temperatures are below zero Fahrenheit most of the time, although no worse than the Antarctic where man has learned to survive. The Mariner 6 and Mariner 7 photographic missions to Mars in the summer of 1969 have shown us that Mars, like the moon, has many giant craters, presumably meteoric in origin. There is also evidence, however, that erosion or wind action have been at

125

work to smooth out some of the rough areas, so that it is not quite as forbidding in appearance as the moon. Although there are icecaps at the poles each Martian winter, it is believed that they are made of carbon dioxide, not water, and are very thin, and that there is very little moisture on the planet. Life may exist, although probably only in the form of primitive lichens and mosses.

At this point, speculation begins. Although they may seem so, these are not just idle fancies, because it is important that we determine the possibilities of life and of adaptation to conditions different from those encountered on earth. When compared with the extremes in possible conditions that may be encountered around the universe, the particular set of circumstances that makes up our earthly environment is a very narrow and special one. Because man feels himself to be unique, he tends to assume that life requires almost exactly this same set of circumstances if ever it has appeared or will appear on any other planet. This assumption may be true, but it seems unlikely. Biologists and chemists are not of one mind on this question, but very little study has yet been done.

Jonathan Leonard's conjecture about what we might find on Mars is an example of the kind of speculation that is a prerequisite to opening up the mind to wider possibilities. Applying freely what we know about chemistry and biology on earth to an assumed set of conditions, Leonard writes:

. . . [Mars] is presumably as old as the earth, and there is good reason to believe that it once had more water on it. Its surface is generally very smooth, and without the eroding action of water it would probably be as jagged as the surface of the moon.

If there were once oceans on Mars, life could develop in them just as it did on earth. It could do so even if the oceans were a great deal smaller and shallower. Life on earth developed in the ocean's surfaces, where the sun penetrates.

Since life on Mars would presumably be as resourceful as it is on earth, it could probably adapt itself to gradually worsening conditions. The departure of the oxygen and most of the water vapor from the Martian atmosphere might not be a killing handicap. There are low forms of life on earth that live without oxygen and do very well. Among them are the familiar yeasts which "breathe" sugar and "breathe out" alcohol. Other types have strange metabolisms that get energy from hydrogen sulfide or iron compounds.

If life on earth can adapt to such odd conditions, it is not too much to expect that life on Mars might learn to get along in an atmosphere without oxygen, even without dependence on any atmosphere. It might, for instance, enclose its living tissues in virtually gas-tight membranes. This would not be very different from the system of earthside plants and land animals that live in desert climates. The active material in their cells consists of substances dissolved in water, but they have no trouble living where water is obtainable only with great difficulty. One further step may have been taken by the Martian plants; that of conserving oxygen as well as water and storing it in their tissues, either as a gas or as some chemical compound rich in oxygen.

If such plants exist on Mars, there is an obvious opening for animals that prey upon them. If the plants contain both oxygen and carbon compounds, the animal that eats them will be eating and breathing too.

Astronomers generally leave such speculation to the space-fiction writers, who are seldom equipped with enough knowledge to make their speculations reasonable. Most of them have peopled Mars with intelligent beings adapted in only one or two ways to the special conditions of the Martian environment. They imagine them with very large lungs to breathe the thin Martian air, and cover them with dense woolly coats to ward off the Martian cold. This is not enough adaptation to permit survival.

If intelligent beings do exist on Mars, they are certainly not at all like the dramatic persons of space fiction. They are just as likely to be disembodied brains like those coldly intelligent creatures that descended on the earth in H. G. Wells' *War of the Worlds*. They may even be clever fungi with sedentary central intelligences directing the operations of far-reaching food-gathering organs. Not enough is known about Mars to give even the sketchiest idea of what its inhabitants are like and how they live or whether they exist at all above the level of lichens or algae.*

In puzzling over these cobweb filaments of thought, it comes home to us how little man still knows. Because we have unlocked so many of the secrets of this earth, past and present, we become complacent about the power and the knowledge being pulled together. Yet we have not begun. Does life always begin in the same way it is presumed to have begun on earth? Will it evolve in the same directions

---

*From Jonathan Norton Leonard, *Flight Into Space* (New York: Modern Library, 1957), pp. 200–202, by permission of Random House, Inc. Copyright 1953 by Jonathan Norton Leonard.

under the same or similar circumstances? Is the evolutionary history of man the only possible route to high intelligence? Can there be a higher intelligence still, and if so, can we even comprehend it? We do not have the inkling of an answer. But we will find clues on or near neighboring planets that are likely to revolutionize our thinking, even if nothing at all of what we call life is found.

Man will learn much by exploring the nearer planets of the solar system; even our barren moon will have surprises for us. The knowledge that will be gained by comparing these completely isolated ecological environments with that of earth will illuminate almost every field of scientific endeavor.

But our own solar system has definite limitations. We will visit Mars and other planets, even establish outposts in self-contained capsule environments on their surface, but the time will soon come when we will push on farther: out. The other worlds that can be the theater for the further realization of man's potentialities are light years away, yet to be known or identified by man.

How far must he go? The Milky Way, we now know, is our view of the galaxy of stars in which our sun plays an incredibly insignificant part. The Milky Way galaxy is roughly the shape of a discus, about 125,000 light years in diameter and about 20,000 light years thick through the middle. It is revolving about its center in a spiral, in which the inner part is moving faster than the outer. Our sun is about 25,000 light years from the center of this discus, traveling at a speed of 137 miles per second in a circular orbit around its center (12 miles per second faster than the general stream of traffic). At this considerable rate of speed (which is about 18 times faster than the now well-known escape velocity from earth), it takes the sun 200 million years to make a single circuit of the galaxy (Payne-Gaposchkin, 1952, p. 30)! In this galaxy, the sun is one among about 100,000 million stars. This immense figure represents the raw material upon which our imagination of other worlds may work. This galaxy is only 1 of an estimated 100 billion similar galaxies within the range of the Palomar telescope, and no one knows how many more may lie beyond; but our own galaxy offers more than enough scope for our expansion.

Are there other planets like the earth, distant worlds, orbiting around other stars? A scant quarter-century ago, astronomers believed there was little likelihood that many other planets existed and that very possibly our solar system with its earth was unique. A popular hypothesis about the formation of the planets depended upon the agency of another star, which passed close enough to the sun so that gravitational attraction pulled large masses from the sun, later to condense into the various planets. In view of the emptiness of space, the near-collision of two stars is what Sir James Jeans described in developing this theory, as "an event of almost unimaginable rarity" (1930, p. 1). This theory gave much solace to those who still wanted to believe that man was a unique creation of God.

In the past few years, Carl Friedrich von Weiszacker and others have returned to a Kantian hypothesis by showing that the sun and planets can be accounted for by gravitational condensation from a rotating gaseous disk. George Gamow discusses this theory in *The Creation of the Universe*:

Only the largest eddies will be kept together by the force of Newtonian gravity, and thus escape subsequent dissolution. Within these eddies the process of dust aggregation will continue at a rapid rate, resulting finally in the growth of planets. Studying in detail the properties of the original solar nebula, and the turbulent motion produced by its rotation, it was possible to obtain the correct sizes of the different planets of the solar system. It was also possible to give a reasonable explanation of the famous Bode-Titius rule of planetary distances, which states that within the planetary family (considering the asteroid ring between Mars and Jupiter as the remains of an old planet) the distance of each member from the sun is approximately twice the distance of the previous one. . . . Such a process of formation results in different chemical constitutions for the smaller and larger planets. While "rim" planets (Mercury to Mars on the inner side, and Pluto on the outer side) never grow massive enough to attract much interstellar gas, and thus remained essentially rocky structures, the "halfway" planets (Jupiter, Saturn, and, to a lesser degree, Uranus and Neptune) grew beyond that limiting size and were able to capture by gravity a lot of the material from the original gaseous shell before it was dissipated into the surrounding space.*

The significance of this new theory has come home to us only in the last few years. Why does it matter whether the planets were formed as a result of an accidental near-collison with another star or by condensation of the rotating gaseous disk itself without outside intervention, particularly as this all happened several billion years ago? It is impor-

*From *The Creation of the Universe* by George Gamow. Reprinted by permission of the Viking Press, Inc.

tant because it means that what we now believe happened to our star, the sun, in this solar system probably happened to many stars throughout the galaxy, and therefore it means that many stars must have a ring of planets around them, distributed proportionally much as they are in our own solar system. Instead of few, if any, other planetary systems in this Milky Way galaxy of ours, the astronomers now believe that there are millions of such systems.

All stars, of course, are not alike. They vary immensely in all their important features. Our sun is fairly typical of an average star. The so-called main-sequence stars run in a continuous series from bright to faint, from hot to cool, from massive to light, and from large to small. The brightest main-sequence stars are 10,000 times as bright as the sun, the faintest perhaps 1/1,000,000 as bright. Their sizes range from 20 times to 1/10 the sun's size, their temperatures from a couple of thousand to a half-million degrees, and their mass from 1/10 to 40 times the mass of the sun. These are the stars that will have planetary systems. For the purposes of this discussion, we need not be concerned about the red giants, white dwarfs, and the other stars not on the main sequence. Despite the wide range in characteristics, there are an incredible number of stars very like our sun (Payne-Gaposchkin, 1952, p. 28).

Is there direct evidence that any other star actually has any planets? New impetus has been given to searches in that direction, and observers have been looking among our stellar neighbors for any evidence that planets do exist.

Some years ago at the Sproul Observatory of Swarthmore College, Peter van de Kamp discovered that Barnard's star (one of the closest stars to earth and only 6.1 light years dis-

tant) did not move through space in a perfectly straight
line. The minute wobbles of Barnard's star led to the conclusion that a planet-sized invisible companion was revolving around this star once every 24 years. Continued observations have disclosed a secondary perturbation, which has
been interpreted to mean that Barnard's star has still another companion planet and that the two planets each approximate the mass of Jupiter, with orbits of 26 and 12
years, respectively. Our observations are not yet subtle
enough to show any planet that Barnard's star might have
so small as earth, but future studies will tell us more.

What are our so-called stellar neighbors in the galaxy?
The triple-star system of Alpha Centauri (seen only in the
Southern Hemisphere) is the nearest, being 4.4 light years
away, which means in astronomical terms that light traveling at 186,000 miles per second will take 4.4 years to reach
the earth from Alpha Centauri. This compares with the approximate eight minutes it takes for the light of the sun to
reach the earth and the less than two seconds it takes for
light to travel between our moon and earth. Put on the 1-
inch scale used above to describe the solar system, Alpha
Centauri is 50,000 miles away, and there is no star we
know of in-between. If the 3-star system of Alpha Centauri
is counted as 1 star, there are 26 stars within a distance of
13 light years from the earth, which puts these stars about 5
light years apart from each other. Most of these stars are
much fainter in absolute brightness than the sun, many of
them not 1/100 as bright. Only two of the nine nearest stars
(other than the sun) are brighter than the sun: Sirius, 26
times as bright, and Alpha Centauri, 1.3 times as bright.

We can only conjecture how many of these neighbors

have planets capable of supporting life. For assuming any planets exist, we know neither what the environments on them may be nor what conditions will permit the beginning and survival of life itself. The number of possible permutations and combinations of conditions necessary for habitability is so great that it is fruitless to speculate at length, at least until we know more about our own solar system. But that some neighboring planets exist and are habitable—although not necessarily inhabited—seems to be a conclusion with a reasonably high order of probability.

Fred Hoyle sums up a discussion of other planetary systems with a view that represents so revolutionary a change from his (and others') position of a few years before that he finds it necessary to be facetious to lighten the impact of its significance:

> Living creatures must, it seems, be rather common in the Universe. It is something of a cosmic tragedy that the distances from one star to another are so vast by ordinary standards that there seems no prospect of one group of creatures being able to establish communication with another. This is a pity, because the supporters of various ideologies after impressing the superior merit of their views on each other (through the aid of fusion bombardment and other massive activities), could proceed to impress themselves on the rest of the Milky Way. Not only this, but the opportunities for tax-collectors would be enormous. With taxes levied on say 250,000,000,000,000,000,000 individuals instead of a mere 2,500 million it would be possible to whack up the defence programme for the Milky Way to something like reasonable proportions. (Hoyle, 1955, p. 105)

Hoyle states today's generally accepted opinion that, based on overwhelming probability, there are bound to be a great many forms of life on a vast number of assumed planets in our galaxy alone. His assumption that distance precludes contact with any of these planets may be correct, but should not be accepted without further study, as I shall attempt to show.

8

Outward Ho!

LET us imagine a prospective flight to a planet of a star 12.2 light years away from earth. Sometime late in the twenty-first century, an expedition will be launched to colonize one of these planets. Today, a century or more before the event, much may be conjectured about the voyage that will start humankind in a new direction with consequences that can only be dimly foreseen. In the present chapter, this incredible journey will be discussed as matter-of-factly as the subject will permit.

By the time of this voyage, man will have been long accustomed to space travel within our own solar system. We will have several well-established colonies on or beneath the surface of the moon, where thousands of earthlings and many of their descendants will be living in an environment shielded from the radiation bombardment of open space and the temperature extremes of the moon's surface. We will also have established a foothold on Mars with a smaller colony, also in an artificial environment. We will have a permanent manned observatory orbiting Jupiter (perhaps on one of its moons) and will have used many unmanned probes to explore the surface of all the other planets. We will know that no planet in our solar system other than earth is more than marginally habitable by man and that there is little prospect that any of these colonies will become more than temporarily self-supporting.

From these colonies, however, man will receive a growing flood of information about the universe beyond. Astronomical observatories on the moon, where they will escape the distortions of the atmosphere that limit our earthly vision of the sky, will have provided mankind with a vivid and detailed picture of the universe.

There are 40 or more stars within 15 light years of our solar system. Let us assume that in the twenty-first century our information discloses that several of these stars have one or more planets that might be suitable for colonization by man. We will be able to identify these planets from our moon observatories. We will have studied the perturbations in the orbit of each star and of the other planets in each system to define precisely the size, mass, and orbit of each planet we find interesting. Intensive analysis of the few rays that reach our instruments will teach us much about these planets. Scanty as the data will be, our analytic techniques will permit us to select several planets as potential candidates for colonization.

In the fourth or fifth decade of the twenty-first century, we will dispatch instrumented space probes out of our solar system to these preselected planets of other stars to obtain more detailed information. Because of the vast distances involved, these space probes will not have time to coast through space to their objective but will be required to accelerate to nearly the speed of light, perhaps using techniques suggested for the colonizing expedition itself.

These planets of other stars will be as much as 15 light years distant from earth, so that a round-trip radio signal traveling at the speed of light would take 30 years. Even if these probes can be accelerated to approach the speed of light for much of their journeys, more than 30 years will elapse between launch and the time the information gleaned on arrival at the destination can reach us on earth.

Let us assume that analysis of the data received later in the century (30 or more years later) shows that a planet of the star Tau Ceti, 12.2 light years distant from our solar system, best meets our specifications and is, in fact, a potentially hospitable new world for man. This planet will be selected for colonization by man. For convenience, let us call this future human home "Olympus."

Several years before the assigned date of departure, all the necessary components of the spaceships for the voyage and all the equipment for the colony will have been built and assembled. The selection and training of the crew that will man this expedition will have been completed, and the prospective colonists will have been chosen and prepared. These preparations will begin on earth, but the final assembly will be accomplished first on the surface of the moon and then in a convenient orbit around it. Finally, at the assigned moment, the engines will be started and the caravan will lift out of moon orbit on a predetermined trajectory.

If the caravan is to reach Olympus in one lifetime or less, speeds approaching the speed of light must be attained because of the vast distance involved. 12.2 light years, being the distance that light travels in that length of time at its constant speed of 186,000 miles per second amounts to 71,700,000,000,000 (71.7 trillion) miles. A spaceship traveling at the escape velocity from earth, 25,000 miles per hour, would therefore reach the neighborhood of Tau Ceti in about 300,000 years. At the slower speeds that are more efficient for coasting between the earth, moon and the local planets, it would take three times as long. Obviously, a faster way must be found.

How will we get there in time? If a spaceship (or a fleet of ships) could have sufficient propulsive power to accelerate continuously to the approximate midpoint of the voyage and thereafter apply the same power to decelerate for the balance of the trip all at the rate, say, of 32 feet per second per second, which is the rate of acceleration of any falling body on earth, the time problem becomes manageable. At this rate of acceleration (1 g), it takes about a year to near the speed of light, measured by time here on earth, and another year to decelerate back down again so that the time to reach Tau Ceti's system would be about 15 years.

How could this be done? Even if a century from now we have developed the most efficient engines we can possibly imagine, relying on nuclear fusion of hydrogen, no spaceship could carry enough fuel to supply the continuous power required for even a tiny fraction of the necessary time. The only alternative we can now imagine is to obtain sufficient fuel enroute. Robert W. Bussard has suggested a possible answer: a ramjet engine with tremendous frontal surface area to suck in enough interstellar gas to propel the ship. So empty is interstellar space, however, as we now calculate, that the ramjet would need for fuel all the gaseous particles in its route in a moving surface area with a diameter of about 1,000 miles. This enormous area would not necessarily be swept up by a material scoop; it could, for example, be covered by a generated magnetic field, which would capture the particles in the path ahead by ionizing them and guiding the ions into the intake area (Shklovskii and Sagan, 1966, pp. 445-446).

If the speed and time problems can be solved, the other technical difficulties of the journey itself will be capable of solution a century hence. In many respects, we can now see the precise directions in which our knowledge and skills must expand if we are to be ready in time. Many scientific breakthroughs will be necessary to make the voyage possible. Even more will be needed to insure a high probability of eventual success. Man's technical ability and knowledge are expanding at an accelerating rate, and I assume that they will continue to expand at this geometric rate during the century ahead. If so, even though the task is huge in scale and extremely difficult and complex, we will be able to accomplish it, if the need is great enough.

When we consider that the Space Age is scarcely a dozen years old and that we are just learning how to reach our own satellite moon, it is not surprising that we have yet to find a feasible way to span distances that are measured in light years. We may discover that a journey to the stars is an impossibility or is too great a task for man ever to accomplish; it is too early to tell. Bussard's conjectured means, however, does not violate any known physical law and involves no recourse to the hyper-drives, fifth dimensions, or other magical solutions of science fiction.

141

In the context of the present accelerating pace of technological development, however, 100 years seems like ample time to prepare for this journey. Only 66 years elapsed between the first manned flight at Kittyhawk and man's landing on his satellite. To scientists of 1900, the present space program would have been at least as incredible as planetary colonization now seems to us, even though those scientists would have grossly underestimated the variety and difficulty of the problems that eventually had to be solved to get as far as the moon. On the other hand, who would have foreseen the development of radio, radar, television, rocket engines and cryogenic fuels, computer technology, the transitor, stainless steel and all the high-alloy metallurgy, and the fields of quality and reliability control and systems analysis, just to name an obvious few, without which a space program would be impossible. Nor can we guess the development of the future. The age of technological breakthroughs has scarcely begun. Our present technology will seem childlike a century from now. Immense as the task is, I firmly believe that this journey will be within man's capabilities by the time another 100 years goes by.

I assume a caravan of seven ships, six of which will have no humans aboard. The first of these will be a scout ship, designed to keep station a few minutes travel time ahead. It will be equipped with instruments to scan the vast emptiness of space through which the caravan must travel; locate and identify every piece of matter that might be a hazard to any ship; plot its speed and trajectory; and, in the once-in-a-million case in which a collision would otherwise occur, it will direct the guidance system of the ship concerned to execute the minimum avoidance maneuver so that the potentially damaging particle will pass it by, even if only by inches. This ship will be the eyes of the fleet, the destroyer escort that guards the big ships from any dangers ahead.

Five of the other six ships will serve only as fuel collectors positioned at the five points of a pentagon (through the center of which the main ship will follow) and will sweep out the space ahead. Each of the five will take a giant core out of the space through which it passes—perhaps by creating a magnetic field, as Bussard suggests; perhaps by some other method we have yet to discover. Each will redirect this material, in ionized form, into the engine intake that it supplies.

The main ship will be a giant vessel, hundreds of feet long; its nuclear engine will be separated by a long boom from the honeycomb of the control, living, working, and storage areas. Perhaps a dozen or so crewmen will be necessary to handle all the necessary controls and chores of the long interstellar voyage. The several hundred prospective colonists will have had their metabolism arrested by freezing (or some other technique yet to be developed) so that they can be stored away like the rest of the baggage until Olympus is reached. In this way, space and food will be conserved. At the same time, the colonists will be able to arrive at their new world without the strain and boredom of the long voyage; they will wake up literally as young as the day they left home years before.

Tau Ceti, as we earthlings see it, is in the constellation Cetus in the southern sky so that the fleet will leave the plane of the ecliptic of our solar system in which its planets circle and will move into interstellar space without passing Mars, Jupiter, or any of the outer planets. Year after year, the seven vessels will accelerate at a constant rate. Space is silent and unbelievably empty. The only physical awareness of speed on the main ship will come from the vibration of the engine transmitted through its frame and the steady gravity provided by the acceleration.

Gradually the sun of our solar system will dim in the distance, until it is just another star in the firmament. After a year or so, the seven ships will be hurtling through space and moving into and collecting the dust and gas of interstellar space at almost the speed of light. Fantastic techniques will be required, perhaps fundamentally related to those used for the fuel collecting itself, to insure that these particles go only into the engine intake and do not burn up ship and crew together. The acceleration will continue, but no matter how much and how long it is applied, the speed of light will never quite be attained, nor can it be.

The voyage will be marked only by monotony. From time to time the engines will probably need attention and may have to be shut down. When this occurs, the ship will coast at the speed it has attained, indefinitely if necessary, and the crew will experience weightlessness until the engines are restarted. Otherwise, nothing will happen; the engines will just bore on and on through the night sky.

Seven or eight years after launch, as the midpoint of the journey is reached, the engines on all seven ships will be shut off for a brief time while the small control jets revolve the ships so that they are facing back toward earth. The engines will then be facing in exactly the opposite direction so that their thrust will start the deceleration process. Because just as much fuel is needed to slow down as to speed up, the fuel collecting devices, however, will remain facing toward

Tau Ceti and continue to scoop up every particle the engines need to keep on firing. During the turnaround, the fleet will coast in a temporarily weightless environment, but the uniform pressure of gravity will be felt again as soon as the engines are restarted.

On and on, the seemingly endless voyage will go. Gradually, as the years roll by, Tau Ceti will become visible as more than another star. Finally, in a process that reverses the original departure, all seven ships will settle into a parking orbit thousands of miles above planet Olympus. Once this is achieved, the control jets of the main vessel will be used to push the whole vast ship into a slow rotation around its own axis thus providing by centrifugal force the minimum artificial gravity needed for a good working environment for humans.

The fleet will reach its destination safely, but it will be months—probably years—before men land on the surface of their intended home.

Great as the risks of the voyage will be, greater dangers will lie ahead. So carefully has the Apollo exploration program been developed that when men finally landed on the moon, there were no surprises. This will not be true when we reach Olympus. Radio communications from the moon take less than two seconds; from Olympus it will take 12.2 years, without any allowance for the time it would take any probes to get there in order to send a message. Of necessity, our information will be scanty and out of date so that the journey into the unknown will involve greater risks than today's near-space ventures, which make use of a step-by-step approach that has helped assure their success.

Now that the fleet has arrived, the work will begin.

Among the dormant colonists, a number of them with special skills will be needed to man the many programs that must be begun, and appropriate controls will be activated to awaken them. Imagine the emotional impact of coming back to life in orbit above a strange, new world. Imagine, also, the shock to the crew (which no preparation can entirely absorb) on seeing these young people rise to life as fresh and youthful as when the trip began, while all these monotonous years have left the crew many years older. We may be sure that the psychologists of the twenty-first century, anticipating this reaction, will insist that the crew should never have met nor have seen any of the colonists before the voyage began.

An immense quantity of new data about Olympus will be collected and analyzed. Much will be learned about the planet, even while the spaceship is in high orbit, by using a variety of detecting instruments, many of them not yet invented today. Assuming that the surface is not totally obscured by clouds, visual data from camera and telescope will be analyzed and reanalyzed to extract information about this future home.

Instrumented probes will be sent to the planet's surface to record temperatures, pressures, composition of atmosphere, and composition of the surface itself, and they will radio this information back to the circling ship. Special rocket probes will descend and return with samples of atmosphere and surface material for laboratory analysis. These samples will include enough material to disclose whether life exists on Olympus and, if so, what its basic molecular structure is. The spaceship will be designed so that such material can be examined and studied in a sterile quarantined area without danger of contaminating the rest of the ship or any of its personnel.

If man is to live and thrive in this new world, it must be much like the earth from which he comes. Gravity on Olympus should not be much greater than on earth; preferably, it would be the same or even a little less. The atmospheric pressure at the surface must be close to the 30 inches of mercury to which humans are accustomed. Olympus will have already passed this test; with the superior instrumentation of a century hence, the expedition's leaders will know that much and far more about their future home before they leave earth and will eliminate from consideration planets that do not qualify. Likewise, they will be able to determine probable temperature ranges not only from direct observation, but from knowledge of the heat put out by the star Tau Ceti, dimensions of the Olympian orbit around Tau Ceti, the planet's own axis and speed of revolution together with calculations from all this data as to how much heat received will be retained.

If Olympus has sufficient mass, its gravity will be strong enough to retain an atmosphere sufficient to capture some of the heat received and to provide a protective blanket against excessive cosmic ray and other dangerous ray bombardment. The nature of this blanket will be vital because protection is not a function of thickness or density of atmosphere alone; it is influenced or even controlled by the existence of an ozone layer to absorb damaging rays.

Olympus may not rotate on its axis at all; it may keep the same face to Tau Ceti throughout its annual orbit. In this unlikely event, the illuminated side will have far higher temperatures than the dark half of the planet and human life may be possible only in the narrow belt of dusk that divides the two zones. Such a nonrotating planet would have far less habitable area, but the countervailing advantage might be the existence of a wider range of habitats from which to select the one most suitable for man. The number of people that the planet can ultimately maintain will not be a significant criterion of desirability.

Assuming gravity, atmospheric pressure, composition, and temperature are within the viable ranges, many other assurances will still be needed. Suppose that the planet is covered with water or some other liquid ocean. Suppose, on the other hand, that no water at all is available, and it is impossible to obtain water in any substantial volume. We will hope that the planet's composition is as much like earth as possible. Aeons of evolution have adapted us and all the ecology upon which we depend to the special conditions of earth and every change from these conditions makes adaptation difficult, if not impossible.

Although the evidence available before the expedition begins will be, by necessity, sketchy and subject to varied interpretations and assumptions, Olympus will be seen as a "green" planet and therefore endowed with abundant plant life. From the evidence as to the age of its parent star, however, it will be thought that Olympus is younger than earth and will not have had time for as much evolutionary development as we have had on earth. It will be expected, therefore, that the plant life on Olympus will be primitive by earthly standards. Whether animal life exists at all, we probably will not know.

The first samples returned to the spaceship by the rocket probes will show the existence of life, a profusion of plant forms, and an abundant bacterial life. We will assume that analysis confirms the data from the early instrumented probe and shows that, like life on earth, life on Olympus is based on the carbon-hydrogen bond and is sufficiently similar to life on earth so that there is hope of compatibility and, thus, survival for the colonists.

In the medical laboratory aboard ship, an elaborate series of tests will determine in detail the interactions between the life forms of earth and Olympus. The bacteria of Olympus will be tested on a variety of artificial human organs, which will act as analogues of different functions of the human body itself. In this way, the consequences of the contacts and interactions will be accurately measured and evaluated. Test animals brought from earth will be awakened from suspended life and used as test objects for all the Olympian bacteria.

It would be amazing if some sharp incompatibilities were not disclosed. We have learned on earth itself that when a disease considered mild among species that have evolved resistance to it is introduced to a country that has never experienced its effect, the results are often catastrophic. The seriousness of this danger will be given prime consideration. Over a period of weeks while lazily rolling in orbit, many such potential hazards will be discovered and studied. A century from now medical science will have a host of tools scarcely hinted at today; the ability to immunize a population against new diseases will be one of them.

One or two bacterial strains, however, will prove so virulent that no prevention or cure seems possible, and medical technicians will confess their helplessness. Yet every problem must be solved if the expedition is not to end in extinction. Biochemists will be asked to fight fire with fire by changing the ecology of Olympus or at least a limited part of its surface to eliminate the toxic substance entirely. Extensive tests lasting weeks, even months (of earth time), will show biochemists that the viral problem can be solved if certain earth molecular forms are introduced to Olympus and are free to propagate at the expense of the more primitive Olympian bacteria, relying on the laws of evolutionary natural selection to do their work. Although all the effects on the planet's ecology cannot be known from the scanty available data, it will be decided that there is no alternative but to make this introduction and to monitor the results as closely as possible.

The chief ecologist will have been poring over the information received about the interrelationships and interdependencies of all life forms that can be identified from the samples brought back to orbit. From this information, a tentative site for the colony will be selected and the spaceship will be brought down to the correct altitude for synchronous orbit stationed above that spot. This will still be far above the highest limits of the planet's atmosphere.

At this point, it will be decided that several humans, sealed and protected in armored space suits, should make a trial landing on the planet's surface to learn more than can be obtained from robot probes. The trip will be made, and the surface will prove hospitable. The group will return and report, from quarantine, sighting a wide variety of plant life and glimpses of one or two primitive forms of animal life.

During this period, the spaceship will radio back to earth a stream of information. Because a round-trip radio signal takes 24.4 years at the speed of light, however, the messages coming in from earth can inform the voyagers only of what has transpired at home in the solar system in the first few years after they began their journey. For all practical purposes, the colonists are on their own.

After four months in Olympian orbit, the campaign of seeding the surface with bits of life from earth will begin. Three years will elapse before the surface ecology begins to feel the effect.

Intense activity aboard ship will continue during this long waiting period. The physical, chemical, biological, ecological, and medical laboratories will be working full time to assemble, analyze, and coordinate enough data to have a full picture of the problems and perils to be faced. Extended trips will be made to the planet's surface, and the information brought back will help to fill out the details of conditions and life on Olympus.

As a result of these studies, it will be decided to introduce various additional forms of earth life, both plant and animal, in a deliberate plan to change the ecology so that it is more suitable for man's colonization. Existing life on the planet will be primitive by our standards, and many Olympian species will be extinguished in competition with the more advanced species from earth.

In fact, the colonists will be prepared, if they find no life on Olympus, to seed the entire planet to provide a total ecology from bare rock. The spaceship will have a storehouse of seeds and a minimum matrix of nutrients, and, there will be a stock of many varieties of small animal life in frozen form, ready to be awakened in a new world if (and only if) the circumstances are right and they are needed. The result could be a simplified version of earth's ecology with a limited but balanced variety of forms of life sufficient to provide a viable environment, at least until more species could be imported from earth.

Today, on earth, we cannot tell and do not know what will occur when life forms that have evolved from the very first molecule in different worlds meet and compete in a single environment. A century from now, we will probably have the benefit of having studied unique although rudimentary life forms on Mars and will have learned whether any compatibility with life on earth is possible. If our studies on Mars disclose that total quarantine between different life forms is necessary forever, then the Olympus we will select must be a lifeless planet that our colonists will then have to endow with selected species from our own abundant variety of forms of life.

Whether our colonists will start from scratch or seek to modify existing life to suit their requirements, let us assume that three years of waiting will be required for the necessary changes on planet to occur, first slowly in one or a few small areas and then rapidly spreading in all directions. All will have to be closely monitored. Three years may not be enough time; today we can scarcely guess.

We can hope, however, that the planet will eventually be ready for human habitation and that the remaining colonists will be awakened and sent down to the surface of the new world to assume the thousand tasks of building a new world. When all of them have landed on Olympus, the main spaceship will be disassembled and landed, as will the other six ships. These ships will no longer have any value in space, but every ounce of material from them will be invaluable in starting this new civilization.

Thus, the colonists will cut the symbolic umbilical cord to mother earth. For many years there will be no possibility of returning to earth and except for twelve-year-old news by radio, there will be no contact at all. The colonists will have no choice but to do the best they can with what they have brought and what they can find in their new home. They will be on their own as no humans have ever been before, and there will be no possibility of rescue.

Thus, man will inhabit his new world. The difficulties will be enormous and the prospects of success will be doubtful. The obstacles that I have touched upon may prove insuperable. Because of unforeseen difficulties the colony may terminate in disaster. We cannot estimate the likelihood of finding a world that can be made into a home for man. A hundred years from now, before such a voyage begins, we will know much more than we do at present, but still not enough.

Is the kind of journey I have just described really possible? Or better, is it realistic to think that it would be possible within the next 100 years? It is always dangerous to make predictions, but this book is essentially an exercise— if not in prediction then in extrapolation—and therefore I must be bold and answer affirmatively while remembering Lewis Mumford's caution that "trend is not destiny." Yes, such a journey will be possible, for in describing it, I have made use only of existing knowledge and technology. I have accepted the laws of physics and have had no recourse to magic forces, quantum jumps, hyper-drives, or similar devices of science fiction. I have simply imagined an expansion of existing knowledge and technology.

Thus far, the imaginary journey has dealt with three

basic problems: obtaining adequate fuel for the voyage (by magnetic collectors), arresting human aging (by cryogenic devices or freezing), and making a strange planet suitable for human habitation by bringing about ecological changes. The solutions proposed are well within the future capability of mankind, if technological progress continues at the present rate—even without allowing for its continued acceleration.

Although there are many technical problems to be solved and some technological breakthroughs to be made, scientists and engineers are already discussing and preparing for space travel within the solar system as though they were simply designing a new and bigger building.

When we turn to transstellar travel, however, the distances involved are so vast that the scale of the difficulties to be overcome soars several orders of magnitude. Even so, most of the basic problems are the same ones experienced in space travel within our own solar system. Among these are other problems that require discussion; some of them have probably occurred to the reader. The first is weightlessness. In outer space there is little or no force of gravity. On the surface of the earth, man, like all living creatures, has evolved to cope with an environment in which there is a strong and constant pull of gravity. He has developed the strength to resist it, which if unused, will wither away. More important, many of his organs are adapted to make use of gravity as an aid in their effective functioning. For example, our sense of orientation depends on gravity's effect on the semicircular canals of the ear. Medical scientists have been studying these problems for years and still have a long way to go before they understand what the effects of weightlessness will be, let alone work out means of adapting man to such effects.

It now appears that for any extended voyages in space it will be necessary to create some degree of artificial gravity as a sure means of solving this problem.

The second problem is man's vulnerability to cosmic rays and to other forms of intense radiation. The earth's atmosphere is a highly efficient blanket protecting life from all but a very small fraction of the high-powered subatomic particles that dart around the universe above at the speed of light. Such ionized radiation is intensely damaging to man, but no effective shielding has yet been discovered that would not increase the weight of any spaceship by many times. Before the first satellite went into orbit, it was believed that the space in our solar system would be largely free of this danger, or at least, that it would be well within tolerable limits. Since the discovery of the Van Allen belts of ionized particles around most of the earth, the problem has taken on a more serious aspect, and the storms of such particles emanating from the sun add another grave danger to the hazards of space travel, even in our own solar system.

Both difficulties are the result of our evolution, and it is worth digressing to explain why this is so. We are all the product of aeons of natural selection in an environment in which gravity has been constant and reliable. When the first creatures came out of the sea, they had to be stronger in structure to cope with gravity's greater force outside the supporting element of water. Not only were the bodies of the land animals developed to resist and work against gravity; their way of life and their very organs became adapted

155

to work with it and use it to assist their tasks. No foresight was involved; evolution reacted to and took advantage of the circumstances as they were.

The problems of weightlessness and vulnerability to ionizing radiation are important, but they are far less severe than those that were faced when life emerged from the sea. Although we do not have millennia to evolve our structure to cope with them, we have the benefit of our burgeoning technology to speed the solution. Clarke compares the transition from sea to air with the one from air to space thus:

> The possible advantages of space can be best appreciated if we turn our backs upon it and return, in imagination, to the sea. Here is the perfect environment for life—the place where it originally evolved. In the sea, an all-pervading fluid medium carries oxygen and food to every organism; it need never hunt for either. The same medium neutralizes gravity, insures against temperature extremes, and prevents damage by too-intense solar radiation—which must have been lethal at the earth's surface before the ozone layer was formed.

> When we consider these facts, it seems incredible that life ever left the sea, for in some ways the dry land is almost as dangerous as space. Because we are accustomed to it, we forget the price we have had to pay in our daily battle against gravity. We seldom stop to think that we are still creatures of the sea, able to leave it only because, from birth to death, we wear the water-filled space suits of our skins.*

---

*From Arthur C. Clarke, *Voices From The Sky*. (New York: Harper & Row Publishers, Inc., 1965), pp. 13-14, by permission of the publishers.

Now that there is the prospect of going into space, we are faced with a complete change in circumstances to which adaptation may prove difficult although not necessarily impossible. The fish is already halfway between us and a weightless world; its biological adaptation to this particular element in the space environment is easier than it would be for us or for any land animal.

The question of cosmic rays is more serious. There is much popular misunderstanding of the effects of ionizing radiation whether from cosmic rays or from products of man-made atomic fission. All such radiation is damaging to life as we know it. Any cell hit by a radiation particle has been hit by a bullet with usually damaging effect. The more cells are hit, the worse is the damage to the organism as a whole. A certain amount of this radiation has always been present in our atmosphere, and because we survive it without apparent adverse effects, this so-called background of normal radiation is considered safe. Similarly, lightning is considered safe because it seldom strikes.

Even when the affected cells are not germ cells, the matter is of direct consequence. If radiating strontium 90, for instance, is absorbed in the system of a growing child when he eats vegetables exposed to atomic fallout, his bone marrow will be affected; the greater the intensity of the radiation, the greater the possibility of contracting leukemia becomes. Although the effect on a large population may be statistically negligible when exposure is slight, it is doubtful that any level above zero is completely safe for all people. The dose may be intense enough to kill almost at once or it may merely shorten life by a few days or hours. In either case, only the exposed individual is damaged.

When germ cells are exposed to ionizing radiation, the problem is more serious. Mutations result; this occurs at every level of radiation. Mutations, as we know, are almost always harmful. The mutation of a particular gene is usually recessive, shows up only in the descendants of the individual exposed, and may not appear for a number of generations. This radiation affects the future of the race, and it is almost impossible to predict when or how it will appear. We do know that there are more than enough mutations in human genes today and that any increase in their number is disadvantageous to our human future. No absolutely safe level exists, and the arguments raging on the subject are often involved in the semantic question, How safe is "safe"? (For a scientific survey of the environmental effects of ionizing radiation, see Handler [1970], pp. 871–876.)

Whether man in space can cope with a potentially higher level of ionized radiation without jeopardizing our future is not yet known. Perhaps from the storehouse of genes available in the human family will come combinations that thrive on these hazards. Only by learning of the lethal effect of DDT on houseflies did we discover that the few survivors happened to have alleles (alternative forms of the same gene) resistant to DDT. These alleles had been present in a small proportion of the species, but had never before had a positive selective value. A less drastic way of identifying the radiation-resistant humans had better be found.

Serious as the problems are, the concentrated attack on them by scientists and doctors all over the world will bring solutions as they are needed, so that travel through space within our solar system will become feasible in the years to come. But this is only the beginning.

Outward Ho!

A few years ago the exploration of our planetary neighbors was itself an exploit far beyond man's wildest dreams. Thus, little serious attention has been given to the even greater difficulties of exploring such planets as may orbit other stars. It is one thing to coast around the solar system at speeds not greatly exceeding the escape velocity of earth by using the orbital speeds of the planets to help propel the rocket from one planet to another at the precise moment that is most advantageous. This can be done with a minimum package of built-in power with all the predetermined amount of fuel for the journey aboard at the takeoff. It is quite another thing to reach the neighborhood of a nearby star, such as Tau Ceti, 12.2 light years away. At the rocket speeds suitable for intrasolar-system travel, this journey would take almost 1 million years. If space travel is to be successful, we will need vehicles that can be kicked up to speeds that are substantial fractions of the speed of light, or the journeys will be virtually endless.

If a constant power source could be developed and used the spaceship could be accelerated at a constant rate (1 g, for example, would be comfortable for earthlings aboard) until the midpoint of the voyage and then decelerated at the same rate for the remainder of the trip (as described in the imaginary journey to Tau Ceti) in far less than a normal lifetime. At higher rates of acceleration and deceleration, the journey would be shorter still. Note also that because the acceleration continues at a constant rate to the midpoint of the journey, the farther away the goal is, the higher speed the vessel will attain.

The star Vega is 27 light years distant compared to Tau Ceti's 12.2 light years. But because of the speeds attained, such a journey to Vega would take less than twice as long as the journey to Tau Ceti.

When we begin serious plans to explore distant star systems, we will take special note of a remarkable effect of Einstein's theory of special relativity: the phenomenon of relativistic time dilation. Time in a moving system runs slower, and this is measured by the proportion $\sqrt{1 - \dfrac{v^2}{c^2}}$ in which v is the velocity of the system and c is the speed of light. This becomes significant only as the speed of light is approached. What does this mean? Carl Sagan explains it:

The passage of time, as measured by the crew of the space vehicle, would be very slow compared with the passage of time required by their friends, relatives and colleagues on their home planet. As the passengers would travel over immense distances of thousands of light years or more at relativistic velocities, they would become only slightly older. . . . Direct experimental confirmations of time dilation itself also exist. For example, the time for an elementary particle called a mu meson to decay at non-relativistic velocities is well known. If, as a result, for example, of the cosmic ray bombardment of the upper atmosphere, a mu meson were to enter the atmosphere of the Earth traveling at a velocity close to the speed of light, but with its ordinary lifetime, it would never reach the surface of the Earth, and would never be detected there. Instead, mu mesons are commonly detected at the surface of the Earth, because the time for them to decay when moving at relativistic velocities is much longer than the time for them to decay at slower velocities. There is no essential difference between biological time and physical time; both are subject to the same physical laws. Aboard a relativistic interstellar space ship, not only would the passengers' clocks move more slowly, their hearts would beat more slowly, their awareness of the passage of time would be retarded. Relativistic interstellar space flight is in fact a kind of metabolic inhibitor, but one that works on the entire spacecraft.*

Let us apply this rule to our examples of Tau Ceti, 12.2 light years distant, and Vega, 27 light years distant. Assuming again a constant 1 g acceleration to midpoint and deceleration thereafter, Tau Ceti would be reached in less than 7 years of the passengers' lives and Vega in little more than 1 year longer. Let us return to Sagan:

> We see that at an acceleration of 1 g, it takes only a few years, ship time, to reach the nearest stars; 21 years to reach the Galactic center; and 28 years to reach the nearest spiral galaxy beyond the Milky Way. Of course, there is no time dilation on the home planet. The elapsed time in years approximately equals the distance of the destination in light years plus twice the time required to reach relativistic velocities. This time, at an acceleration of about 1 g, is close to one year. For distance beyond about 10 light years, the elapsed time on the home planet in years roughly equals the distance of the destination in light years. Thus, for a round trip with a several-year stopover to the nearest stars, the elapsed time on Earth would be a few decades; to Deneb, a few centuries; to the Vela cloud complex, a few ten thousands of years; to the Virgo cluster of galaxies, a few tens of millions of years; and to the immensely distant Coma

*From I. S. Shklovskii and Carl Sagan, *Intelligent Life in the Universe* (San Francisco: Holden-Day, Inc.), p. 442, by permission of the publisher.

161

cluster of galaxies, a few hundred of millions of years. Nevertheless, each of these enormous journeys could be performed within the lifetime of a human crew, because of time dilation on board the spacecraft. (Shklovskii and Sagan, 1966, p. 443)

The crew of the spaceship hurtling toward Olympus would benefit from time dilation by aging less than 7 years on the voyage that, from the point of view of either the people left on Earth or a hypothetical observer on Olympus would have taken about 15 years.

Science fiction writers, fretting about the limitations of the speed of light for space travel, have turned to the hyper-drive and other fictional devices to get around the universe more rapidly. There is no physical basis for believing the speed of light can be exceeded; in fact, we are as certain as we can be about any physical law that it cannot. Our plans must be laid on the basis of traveling at some pace less than 186,000 miles per second, whether we like it or not.

An alternative to travel at close to the speed of light is a more moderate speed attaining perhaps twice escape velocity or about 14 miles per second; allowing for gradual acceleration at this end and gradual deceleration at the other, this would give an average speed of about 11 miles per second. But when one computes that at such speed we will require over 150,000 years to reach our neighbor Tau Ceti, the trip seems absurd. There are space enthusiasts who believe it would be feasible to equip a spaceship the size of a small planet and send it off with a whole colony of people, to live en route for generation after generation, until that ultimate date thousands of years hence when a landing could be made on a perhaps inhospitable and uninhabitable distant shore. It would seem that this "generation travel" is a desperate attempt to escape the speed and distance problem. If the human race can provide no better road to its expansion than to doom countless generations to such a voyage, we are better off taking our chances here on earth.

Another method of getting human beings across the immense distances of the trackless sky is to deep-freeze all the passengers for the duration of the journey so that the original group, after spending thousands of years in cold storage, can be automatically awakened just in time to set foot on the new world chosen as their destination. This rather terrifying method, now popular with science fiction writers, may well prove medically feasible in the near future. Present medical technology seems far enough advanced so that it is not unreasonable to plan on using deep-freezing even when it is not absolutely necessary for the feasibility of the trip but simplifies a number of logistic and social problems (as in the imaginary journey to Tau Ceti).

The problems of generation travel (without freezing) increase with the length of time the voyage takes. These problems, which have been discussed at length by others, range from the physical difficulties of maintaining a complete and self-sustaining ecology, weightlessness, cosmic rays, and deterioration of unused faculties to the social and psychological problems of confinement for years under conditions highly abnormal for human beings. They are important and difficult problems; some of them are already under scientific investigation, and it may be expected that satisfactory solutions will be forthcoming. This statement is not intended to deprecate the scientific contribution that will be made, for most of the problems would have been classified as impossible of solution a few years ago, and there is a strong temptation to keep many in that category up to the minute that a breakthrough is made.

Serious as they are, however, the problems of the journey are secondary to those of living on a new world. The voyage is only a means to a goal. The emptiness of space will teach us little that cannot be learned from our own solar neighborhood, for astronomers tell us that the composition of matter throughout the universe our telescopes can see is fairly uniform.

But a very precise and complicated set of circumstances is required for man to adapt himself easily to a new physical world. True, he can bring much of his necessary environment with him and protect himself in a capsule from the adverse elements he encounters, but in the long run he must either adapt to the circumstances he finds or—and this may be easier—change the circumstances to suit his requirements.

Many factors in our earthly life are taken so much for granted that we give them no thought, yet these are the very ones that are basic to success. An example is the relation between size and efficiency in the environment. Life is adjusted to the constant force of gravity on earth. The process of natural selection has balanced out the qualities in myriad species to suit this constant force on the land, in the water, and in the air.

Size is not a simple one-for-one proportion. If each of us were to double our height, our skin area would increase by the square of the increase in height and our mass would increase by the cube. The strength of a structural member, such as a bone, is proportional to its cross-sectional area, but the weight of the body it supports increases with the mass, which is the cube of the linear dimension rather than the square.

Every terrestrial animal has evolved in accordance with mathematical laws that determine its most efficient size and shape, taking into account the strength of gravity on earth.

I cannot resist quoting here from J. B. S. Haldane:

> Let us . . . consider a giant man sixty feet high—about the height of Giant Pope and Giant Pagan in the illustrated "Pilgrim's Progress" of my childhood. These monsters were not only ten times as high as Christian, but ten times as wide and ten times as thick, so that their total weight was a thousand times his, or about 80 to 90 tons. Unfortunately, the cross sections of their bones were only a hundred times those of Christian, so that every square inch of giant bone had to support ten times the weight borne by a square inch of human bone. As the human thigh bone breaks under about ten times the human weight, Pope and Pagan would have broken their thighs every time they took a step. This was doubtless why they were sitting down in the picture I remember. But it lessens one's respect for Christian and Jack the Giant Killer. (Haldane, 1956, p. 952)

If, therefore, the force of gravity on earth were doubled, many animals (man, in particular) would have to be drastically redesigned. The average human, therefore, would have to be short and squat, with a much heavier bone structure to get around as a two-legged creature. It is more likely that he would need the stability of four legs to carry the load with any efficiency or freedom. More energy would be required to fuel this revised creature, who would need more food, more blood, and larger lungs. If, on the other hand, gravity were cut in half, evolution would favor the tall and thin. (In *On Growth and Form* [1961], D'Arcy Wentworth Thompson gives us a penetrating discussion of this factor in natural selection.)

Many organs of the body evolved to the only size appropriate to do a job and would be less efficient or break down entirely if they were much larger or smaller. The dimensions of the rods and cones of the eye, for instance, are optically limited by the interference patterns of the waves of light, which set limits on the proper size to produce a clear image. An elephant's eye is bigger than a squirrel's for the former must scan a larger field of vision, but the difference in eye size is not proportionate to the difference in size between the two animals.

When we select a planet that can become a future home for man, therefore, among the first considerations will be its mass—in other words, its total weight. This, together with its radius, will determine the force of gravity on its surface. If it is greater than on our world, man's physical structure would have to be strengthened so that he could stand and walk erect. If it is much lighter than ours, the problem is less serious, but it would still mean that much of our strength needed to cope with our present gravity environment would become unnecessary and atrophy.

This new world would require a solid surface as a foundation for our activity, yet the atmospheric pressure at that solid surface must be not much more than the 30 inches of mercury we experience here. Some planets may be entirely liquid, either water or something else; others, like Jupiter, may have such a deep atmosphere that the surface of the rocky core is under atmospheric pressures that would be intolerable for man.

The atmosphere itself must be viable, with an adequate percentage of oxygen and with no gases toxic to our delicate systems. The temperature must be within a range man can endure, which limits it to from 0° F. to a little over 100° F. The atmosphere must provide the blanket that prevents wide fluctuations in temperature and also protects our delicate organism from cosmic rays and other high-energy particles.

The planet must have as a source of heat and light a star that is reliable and stable. This eliminates pulsating stars, most double and multiple star systems, dying red giant stars, and a host of others.

Twenty years ago, astronomers believed that the number of planets in existence in the universe was few compared to the number of stars and that among such planets the possibilities of finding one fulfilling the conditions above were fantastically remote. Today, post-von Weiszacker, so to speak, the reverse is true. It is considered likely that most stars have planetary systems; that the distribution of the planets around each star comparable to our sun will, following the Bode-Titius rule, be much the same as in our system; and that the probabilities of finding one or two planets in each such system that fulfill most of the conditions we have enumerated is amazingly high.

But there are many other preconditions. This planet must have an organic ecology into which man can fit without being destroyed. Plant life of some kind, following the same

carbon cycle basic to vegetation as we know it, is needed
not only for food but for a continuing source of free oxygen, which would otherwise gradually escape into space.
Biochemists have more and more clues as to how life originates and know that the change from inorganic to organic
can be explained in chemical terms. Such being the case,
given the right conditions and adequate time, life will have
originated on other worlds as it has apparently originated
here.

This life will take other forms on other worlds, starting
from the lowly virus, now thought to be the missing link between life and nonlife, to bacteria, fungi, plants, animals,
and perhaps intelligent creatures that might be called
"men." These differences in life forms will cause extreme
difficulty to invading man. At the cellular level, how can we
imagine the destructive organic forces to which we may be
exposed? The two forms of life may prove completely in-
compatible. This may be a two-edged sword; the germs we
bring to that world may exterminate the very life we expect
to depend on there. Rather than make the evolutionary leap
to adapt to these new surroundings, man may find it easier
to occupy completely barren worlds and import to them all
the forms of life necessary for his existence. Thus, he could
presumably create an ideally balanced environment, if such
a thing could ever exist.

Man may have to cope with hostile creatures. If they are
animals and are inferior to man in intelligence, man with
his weapons will be able to cope with any situation that
might arise. If we find intelligence, unless we happen by remote chance to hit upon a civilization as primitive as ours,
it will probably be too mature to think in terms of force.

Here the writers of pseudo science fiction have led us astray, for they portray on every conceivable world throughout the galaxy creatures amazingly like men in appearance, highly superior in technology with all kinds of mysterious occult powers, but with the emotional maturity of eight year old children.

What kind of beings may we expect on these other worlds? We may assume that life on other worlds is also a product of the evolutionary process and that natural selection has set the directions of its development, at least until the time that it achieves a level of intelligence and technology that permits the imposition of artificial influences upon its evolutionary course. If this is the case, until a civilization attains a technical competence comparable to ours, the laws of Darwinian evolution will apply as well there as here. This means, for example, that the selection process will insure that each species that survives has achieved the balance between courage and caution that best permits it to walk the tightrope of its particular environment and make, on the average, the best decision as to when to stand and fight and when to run away. We may have to learn how it tells the difference.

When we first encounter beings of superior intelligence (and the odds seem to me to be in favor of this ultimately coming about), we may expect the difference in intelligence to be immense. When we consider the pace of man's advance and conjecture about the level he may attain in 10, 100, 1,000, or 100,000 years from now, we realize that in the several billion years that our full inorganic and organic evolution has required, man's entire history is but a fraction of a second and that the chance of hitting upon another world at precisely the same stage is remote beyond all imagination. If the inhabitants of that world are superior, our power will be like a bow and arrow against a guided missile.

We can hope that such other-worldly beings will be above conflict and tolerant of our frailties and stupidities. If we go forth with conquest in mind, we deserve any fate we encounter. If we are looking for knowledge and self-improvement, we may hope for acceptance on that basis and achieve a higher mental stature because of it.

9

The Day After Tomorrow

WHY should any man be willing to venture out into the vast, cold darkness of space and leave behind, perhaps forever, this beautiful world? This is a truly awesome undertaking. It will mean complete and probably permanent separation from the earth that has been his home. It will be uncomfortable, lonely, boring, and hazardous in the extreme.

Space travel to possible planets circling another star is a vastly different project from exploration of the other planets in this, our solar system, just because of the immense distances involved.

What kind of a creature would condemn itself to this kind of life and death, immured in a flying casket, going nowhere? Would he not prefer even solitary and lifelong confinement in the deepest, darkest dungeon on this earth, as a fate far less severe? In my opinion, there are many who would not; in fact, there will be many men and women who will choose this most onerous and permanent exile in preference to all the palaces and pleasures this world can offer. It is this very quality in man that sets him apart from other animals and makes him great.

Although most of us would be appalled by the terrors of space and prefer the bucolic pleasures of a sedentary life, many have the inner fire that inspires them to be selfless instruments of man's greater glory, at any sacrifice. Nor are they fanatics. They must be strong, stable, intelligent people, truly healthy organisms. Only the best will be able to endure the hardships and maintain the discipline necessary to success. We have never lacked volunteers for dangerous missions of any kind, and they will be among the best of our youth.

Carsbie Adams has this to say in *Space Flight*:

[The] motive is [man's] pioneering instinct. Space travel offers a permanent outlet for that intense desire to "see what's over the next hill." Space travel is now the only form of "conquest and empire" compatible with civilization.

There is yet another drive associated with this "aggressive drive," as was once stated by the anthropologist J. D. Unwin: "There is no trace of any display of productive energy which has not been preceded by a display of expansive energy." Sir James Frazer further stated, "Intellectual progress which reveals itself in the growth of arts and sciences . . . receives an immense impetus from conquest and empire." Consequently, we may assume that with space travel and the expansion of the world's mental horizons may come the greatest outburst of creative activity this world has ever known. (C. Adams, 1958, p. xi)

What does all this wild talk about colonizing other worlds in remote stellar systems really lead to? Is this anything more than a fantastic dream of what might happen thousands or millions of years from now? Serious discussion of the consequences of such adventures is purely academic unless there is some possibility of success within a reasonable period of time.

I believe that the odds are in favor of such success, not millennia hence, but in the near future. Of course, this statement cannot be proved. But the trend of our technology is clear, and history has shown that in our civilization obstacles to scientific success are almost always overcome more rapidly than scientists and technicians predict. The greatest obstacle—the only major one to which we do not already hold the key—lies in the vast distances between our solar system and our neighboring stars. This may remain a stubborn problem, but it is difficult to believe that when we are ready in all other respects, ways will not be found to boost spaceships to speeds that will make generation travel unnecessary.

The necessary muscle to achieve almost any goal is available, and full use awaits more subtle methods of extracting and redirecting this power and the development of specific tools to perform the variety of jobs that will need to be done. If our present momentum continues without serious interruption, all this can and will be done within a century or even less.

Man will find that the know-how for successful space

travel will become a secondary problem. I do not underestimate the difficulties; they are far greater than our early successes would lead us to believe, but so are our potential technical capabilities. The likelihood of reaching and establishing any viable foothold elsewhere in our universe may seem small indeed, but we have little alternative. We must try and try immensely hard if man is to remain man and not return to animality.

The determination of what we want to achieve and why we want to achieve it will require far more serious concentration, and it is none too soon to begin the study of this problem.

Primarily because of the scientific discoveries of the past one or two generations, our problems as a species have increased and we have become more aware of them. We are intensely aware of our power to destroy civilization and even mankind itself with the nuclear bomb. We are aware of the dangers of our expanding population and its effects on the kind of lives we will be able to lead. We know that our burgeoning technology is leading to a machine age with implications we can scarcely imagine. We are more aware than ever of the contradictions and tensions within our own nature, and we know that they are in large measure an instinctual heritage from our animal forebears. Finally, as Jean-Paul Sartre saw so clearly, we are beginning to recognize that we have nothing but ourselves to rely on. When we are mature enough to accept that fact, we can develop a humanism adequate for the age in which we live.

Because of these dangers and because of our inner needs, we must escape from this closed system on earth. A number of modern philosophies of history assume a closed system, and this premise profoundly influences their conclusions. Until recently, there was no reason to doubt that the human race is confined to the surface of our planet. As Western civilization expanded over the globe, it became apparent that there was a definite and measurable limit to the area man could occupy; he was coming closer to filling up an area not capable of expansion. In addition, it was known that because the earth is satellite to a star with a limited amount of fuel, the ultimate though distant end of life on earth is assured extinction.

Even the recently recognized possibilities of escape into space do not necessarily change the assumption that the system, although vastly larger than it was previously thought to be, is ultimately finite. The discoveries of modern science focused man's attention and hopes on the physical world at the same time it set definite boundaries to them. We are still held within the laws of physics. The speed of light is the ultimate speed, beyond which nothing may go. The second law of thermodynamics tells us that the entire universe will eventually run down like a clock and come to a complete stop. The concept of curvature of space leads to a possibility, still to be determined, that space is finite rather than infinite. All the universe, like our little world, therefore, may be a closed and eventually dying system. (New theories of a pulsating universe do not change this conclusion for man.)

The realization that these firm walls exist is reflected openly or implicitly in the work of philosophers of history. Almost without exception, they have assumed that mankind's principal future is here on earth, where the limits of the closed system are already at hand. These thinkers differ in the rationales they use and in their descriptions of the ultimate course of history, but they are largely purveyors of gloom.

Spengler finds no escape from endless cycles of rising and falling civilizations set in an unchanging pattern and for him the immediate future is linked to a decaying universal world state. Toynbee clings to the belief that man can escape from this same cyclical form, hoping that the small creative minority of mankind will lift the race up to a higher level through transfiguration, but he cannot hide his fears that the uncreative mass of humanity will fail to respond to the prods and inspiration of the few. He leaves me the impression that the eventual result will be defeat. Pierre Teilhard de Chardin has a glimpse of an expanding future for our species (*The Phenomenon of Man*, 1959), but only by finding a direction and purpose in evolution that I fail to see.

Seidenberg makes the case for the closed system most explicit by arguing that the inevitable triumph of intelligence over instinct will eventually freeze society in a perfected superorganization without a history, under the influence, if not the domination, of the ultimate in machinery. Charles Galton Darwin believes, on the contrary, that intelligence will never win out over instinct. He maintains that man will never solve the population problem; that he will always be the victim, not the master, of his environment.

No one can deny the importance of the laws of physics in estimating what may be expected in the future. We ignore them at our peril. But we may be premature in letting them box in our imaginations completely. There is too much that we do not yet know about the universe. Alfred North Whitehead once said:

The Universe is vast. Nothing is more curious than the self-satisfied dogmatism with which mankind at each period of its history cherishes the delusion of finality of its existing modes of knowledge. Sceptics and believers are all alike. At this moment scientists and sceptics are the leading dogmatists. Advance in detail is admitted; fundamental novelty is barred. This dogmatic common sense is the death of philosophic adventure. The Universe is vast. (Whitehead, 1954, p. 7)

Henry Adams took the lead in applying the laws of science to a philosophy of history, and his contribution was inestimable. But we should be chastened by the experience of his later years. Based on the then (1910) accepted scientific evidence, it was believed that the sun was rapidly cooling down because of an exhaustion of its fuel in a short-range demonstration of the effect of the second law of thermodynamics. On this basis, Adams foresaw a rapid decline of civilization and an early end to man. In "A Letter to American Teachers of History" in *The Degradation of the Democratic Dogma* (1949), he read the obsequies too soon.

If we assume a closed system for the future, then we will doubtless move toward it along the asymptotic curve described by Seidenberg. When we reach it, we will achieve rigidity and perfection, which is synonymous with death. But if we move out into space, the limits are so far away that they are almost meaningless.

What will the conquest of space do for man? The possibilities can be little less than infinite, and even if space itself should prove finite, no limit may ever be reachable. Our imaginations are too constricted by the tiny world that is all we know to be able to define even the nearest of the possibilities of the universe for man.

As a being subject to the laws of biological evolution, man on other worlds may diversify into forms far different from his aspect here. In evolutionary practice, such opening up of new environments has always favored the efflorescence of new variations, sometimes higher and more advanced than any before. Under the stimulus of new opportunities and different circumstances, it is possible that many new and different kinds of supermen may develop. The special conditions of each of the new worlds and the vastness of the space between them will combine to create semi-isolated societies, each coping with its problems and finding its expression in different forms. These are the circumstances under which evolution, both biological and cultural, is most creative.

In his monumental work on the cycles of history, Toynbee stresses that a new civilization does not spring from the ashes of the old, but instead rises on "new ground" far from the center of the civilization to which it is apparented. This "stimulus of new ground" is a subject of study by Toynbee, and he emphasizes that migration overseas to a new scene of endeavor separated by great distance from the source of culture is a special and extra stimulus. A new, isolated land puts to the test the capabilities of the migrants, who find themselves forced to improvise solutions to new problems without help from the motherland. They respond to the challenge or they do not survive.

While the new civilization on new ground is growing, the old civilizations slow to a halt. In a mature and possibly disintegrating civilization, the weight of custom and "the intractability of institutions" is a drag on creativity; this heavier and heavier web of organization and calcified structure tends to slow up the civilization's forward momentum and eventually brings it to a stop. As past civilizations declined and fell, new areas of growth were found outside the geographical scope of the dying cultures. In future generations, when Western civilization becomes world-wide in all its aspects, no place will remain on planet earth from which a new and different civilization might emerge.

The stimulus of solving the problems of living on a different planet, provided that the colony is able to take root and overcome the crushing burdens of establishing itself, will generate new ways of life that will contribute to the richness of man's history and potential future. Even though the parent culture here on earth may be able to avoid stagnation, the freedom to create afresh will make the successful colony the likely breeding ground for a new and different society that will outlast and outshine the parent civilization. The problems of the space colonist in coping with an alien world will at first prevent attention to any subject except stark survival, but once he gains control over his environment, the freedom from the incubus of forms, laws, customs, institutions, habits, and cliches of thought of the highly developed Western civilization, now far away cross the void of space, will permit the development of new and fresh solutions to the problems of life.

In this new and difficult world, the mother country on earth will soon seem remote and unreal. In the face of the unique and overpowering problems of adjusting to a harsh and unnatural environment, the space colonists will be drawn close to each other, regardless of nationality. With vast distances separating them from home, communications will be slow and fragmentary. Although for a long time massive support will be needed from earth to maintain these colonies, the support will doubtless seem misdirected, inadequate, and always too late. The governments on earth will not and, in the nature of things, cannot be expected to understand why the colonists complain that they are not getting what they so desperately need. Assume, for example, that both the United States and the Soviet Union found independent colonies on Mars and support them from earth. Even across this relatively short distance in space, control cannot be effectively exercised. If and when the colonists attain self-sufficiency, remote loyalties to flag and country are likely to be subordinated to the bond of shared hardship and labor in a common task. Here will be found the locus of the new civilization with the vigor and imagination to surpass the old.

As a parent species, man will find his highest expression in the richness and variety of species and cultures that will spring from the parent stock. Here he will find the answer to the biological stalemate that may otherwise overtake him. Only by this means can the probable deterioration of the human species be prevented—by providing the tree of evolution with new branches that can continue to climb long after the parent trunk may have ceased to grow or died out entirely. A special form of selection will give this growth an impetus at the very start, for it is certain that only the best specimens of humankind will make the journeys into space.

In space colonies, small isolated groups will be the laboratories in which social and biological evolution can develop most rapidly. Man will be able to renew his waning biological inheritance of altruism in the small group, where alone it has positive selective value. The many circumstances so different from our own will offer countless environments in which a host of diverse cultures can flower.

Perhaps man is already too overspecialized to survive on other worlds. Many lower forms of life on earth would thrive within a greater range of environments than man could. The humble but incredibly tenacious cockroach, for example, could probably survive on Mars with no artificial aids at all. But man need not conform entirely to his circumstances; fortunately, he can make the situation fit his needs. Here lies his greatness and his hope. That product of his brain, the machine, makes adaptation possible and makes him the potential pilot of the evolutionary process rather than its hapless victim.

Finally, there is the defensive argument that we will no longer be "staking all on one card." If we consider the likelihood that some careless or vicious hand will one day pull the trigger that will spread atomic radiation over our entire world and wipe out the results of aeons of painful evolution, then we must also recognize the need for an insurance policy on the life of the race. Placing some of its members beyond the reach of a single cataclysm would constitute such insurance. Unless we do this, the survival of the human species is doubtful. For this reason alone, space colonization is necessary.

Colonization of other worlds will end the stalemate of the closed society. Reaching out into interstellar space, seeking new worlds light years away, man will find new meanings and purposes in existence. Who can guess what wonders may be revealed to him? We are like fish trying to visualize the world above the water; our imaginations are inadequate to guess what we are likely to find. Opening these new frontiers will be a marvelous stimulus to imagination. Our thoughts will vault to the stars. Arthur C. Clarke reminds us:

> Whether the population of the Solar System becomes ten million or ten thousand million is not, fundamentally, what is important. There are already far too many people on *this* planet, by whatever standards one judges the matter. It would be no cause for boasting if, after some centuries of prodigious technical achievement, we enabled ten times the present human population to exist on a dozen worlds. The importance of planetary colonization will be in the variety and diversity of cultures which it will make possible. . . . It will be fascinating to see what effects this will have on human character, thought and artistic creativeness.*

In space, there is great hope for the human race. Man is the product of change, and he must continue to change. He should be only a step in the process of evolution, not its end product. We cannot let this process come to an untimely end. We should welcome our role as a tiny but important dynamic force in a constantly changing continuum and play this role to the hilt, making full use of our best and highest abilities.

Some people argue that until man has learned to control himself and his own passions, he should not think of any further expansion in his physical powers. Many maintain that technological progress should be stopped until our own

---

*From Arthur C. Clarke, *The Exploration of Space*. (New York: Harper & Row Publishers, Inc., 1951), pp. 185-186, by permission of the publishers.

nature can catch up with it. Actually, the question is academic. Such progress will not stop. It would be easier to throw a lasso around the sun.

But academic or not, the argument is fallacious, because it is through technology that man has his best opportunity to improve and elevate his nature. Want and degradation are the source of much of man's evil, and technology offers man the greatest hope of eliminating them. It also offers the possibility of raising man above himself and some day making him better than he is or can now be. One suspects that many who wish science to call a halt are more interested in taming man than in educating him for a life of opportunity. And as Raymond Queneau said, "The people who whine about naughty robots and inhuman machinery have never proved anything except their own lack of imagination and fear of liberty" (cited in Jean Rostand, *Can Man Be Modified?* [1959]).

The creative minority responsible for all man's advances are unwilling to wait for the masses to catch up. And if they do wait, it will be too late. Whether we will avoid self-obliteration is not yet clear, but a halt in scientific development would not improve our chances. Our main hope lies in pressing on relentlessly through the danger period into a safer and more intelligent time beyond.

If we do push on—and we must—the earth cannot hold the expansive powers of mankind for many more years. The need to break through this new frontier is growing fast, and this need will push us toward successful means. It is more than desirable; it is necessary to man's future that representatives of our species travel to and colonize other planets, even in other solar systems.

In this troubled world, beset with seemingly insoluble problems, it is natural that we daydream about relief from present ills in talk of other worlds. Man has always sought escape from the harsh realities of life in dreams of other worlds. But the exploration of space is not a form of escapism. Its major importance will be in the creation of more and bigger problems, not in the solution of old ones. Man will undertake the challenge so that he may whet his knife against a harder stone.

Spreading out into new worlds will have a profound effect on those who remain on earth. Most immediate will be the greater scientific knowledge that must result from space exploration. Our knowledge of the universe is being increased by every probing step into the outer blackness.

Once astronomers are able to mount telescopes in orbit around the earth so that their view is no longer obscured by our shimmering atmosphere, new fields of knowledge will open up. The origins of our solar system and of the universe as a whole may become clear to us, and this will help us to evaluate our own position in the span of time. No longer will man's vision be limited to what he can see from one tiny point in the universe. As his mobility increases, he will look around the corners that now obscure his view and move closer to any object that interests him to learn what the long view will not tell him.

Physicists may well find the answers to many unresolved questions. What is the nature of gravitation? What are the smallest particles? What more can we learn about the character and properties of light? Which of our physical laws will survive an intense reexamination? In the virtually complete vacuum of space, free from the flux of variables ever present on earth, physical studies and experiments could achieve an accuracy impossible on earth.

There is not a science—chemistry, geology, biology, or any of the others—that will not be boosted to a new height by the information that may be reasonably expected even from the earliest explorations. The greatest single impact may well come from the analysis of the first life found outside our earth, even if it is only the presumed simple lichens of Mars. Does life elsewhere begin in the same way that it began here? Will organic chemistry always be based upon the chain of carbon compounds, or are there other combinations of elements that under different conditions can be the source of life? Does life tend to evolve along the same lines everywhere, or will we find a diversity beyond belief? I doubt that the earthly way is the only way, but until this can be proved by at least one example from another world, we cannot imagine that any other way is possible.

The big gains will come from the unexpected. There are bound to be immense surprises that will have unforeseen impacts on the lives of every member of the human race. All we can be sure of is that the world will be a far different place as a result, even though we do not know what the changes will be.

The great stimulus to the imagination of those who stay behind will help to keep this world from cultural petrifaction. Broadening the perspective of life will lift the spirit of mankind above the problems of the hour. This will be the most valuable benefit of all, worth far more than any material gift that the space travelers may bring back. Clarke sums up this hope:

185

These new frontiers are urgently needed. The crossing of space—even the mere belief in its possibility—may do much to reduce the tensions of our age by turning men's minds outwards and away from their tribal conflicts. It may well be that only by acquiring this new sense of boundless frontiers will the world break free from the ancient cycle of war and peace. One wonders how even the most stubborn of nationalisms will survive when men have seen the Earth as a pale crescent dwindling against the stars, until at last they look for it in vain.*

Perhaps the greatest possibility is that somewhere out beyond we may find an intelligence as great or greater than ours. From what we know of the astronomical universe it seems likely that there are many worlds at least as advanced as we hold our world to be, even in our own galaxy. What greater moment can be imagined than that instant when soul converses with soul across the limitless void? Will man be speechless before something superior beyond his dreaming? Let us have enough faith in man to believe that he will have something of value to offer.

The astronomical discoveries beginning with Copernicus showed that man was no longer the center of the universe; he was merely a speck in the eternity of time and space, which has no center. Is it not possible that these discoveries, so recent in the endless stretch of time, while showing man how small he is, gave him an intimation of how big he might become? Who can guess what knowledge and greatness he may attain?

---

*From Arthur C. Clarke, *Interplanetary Flight* (New York: Harper & Row Publishers, Inc., 1960), p. 145. Reprinted by permission of the author and the author's agent, Scott Meredith Literary Agency, Inc.

Bibliography

Adams, Henry. *The Degradation of the Democratic Dogma*. New York: P. Smith, 1949 (reprint of 1919 edition).
————. *Mont St. Michel and Chartres*. Boston: Houghton Mifflin, 1925 (reprint of 1905 edition).
————. *The Education of Henry Adams*. Boston: Houghton Mifflin, 1918.
Adams, Carsbie, C. *Space Flight*. New York: McGraw-Hill, 1958.
Adler, Irving. *Thinking Machines*. New York: John Day, 1961.
Adler, Mortimer. *The Difference of Man and the Difference It Makes*. New York: Holt, Rinehart and Winston, 1967.
Alland, Alexander, Jr. *Evolution and Human Behavior*. Garden City, N.Y.: Natural History Press, 1967.
Anderson, Poul. *Time and \Stars*. New York: Doubleday, 1964.
————. *Is There Life on Other Worlds?* New York: Crowell, 1963.
Arbib, Michael A. *Brains, Machines and Mathematics*. New York: McGraw-Hill, 1964.
Ardrey, Robert. *The Social Contract*. New York: Atheneum, 1970.
————. *The Territorial Imperative*. New York: Atheneum, 1966.
————. *African Genesis*. New York: Atheneum, 1961.
Asimov, I. *I, Robot*. Garden City, N.Y.: Doubleday, 1966. (a)
————. *The Universe*. New York: Walker, 1966. (b)
Bates, D. R. (ed.). *The Earth and Its Atmosphere*. New York: Basic Books, 1957.
Bates, Marston. *The Forest and the Sea*. New York: Random House, 1960.

187

————. *The Prevalence of People.* New York: Scribner, 1955.

Beadle, George Wells and Muriel. *The Language of Life.* Garden City, N.Y.: Doubleday, 1966.

Becker, Carl Lotus. *Progress and Power.* New York: Knopf, 1949.

Bellamy, Edward. *Looking Backward.* New York: Modern Library, 1951.

Bergson, Henri Louis. *Creative Evolution.* New York: Modern Library, 1944.

Berkeley, Edmund C., and Wainwright, Lawrence. *The Computer Revolution.* Garden City, N.Y.: Doubleday, 1962.

Bernstein, Jeremy. *The Analytical Engine.* New York: Random House, 1964.

Bevan, Edwyn. Letter to Arnold Toynbee in Toynbee, Arnold, *A Study of History.* London: Oxford University Press, 1955. V: 9.

Bitterman, M. E. "The Evolution of Intelligence," *Scientific American,* Vol. 212 (January 1965).

Bonnor, William. *The Mystery of the Expanding Universe.* New York: Macmillan, 1964.

Brown, Harrison. *The Challenge of Man's Future.* New York: Viking, 1958.

Bury, John Bagnell. *The Idea of Progress.* New York: Dover, 1955.

Butler, J. A. V. *Inside the Living Cell.* New York: Basic Books, 1959.

Button, J. S., Jr. "Electronic Device Simulates Processes of Human Brain," *Aviation Week,* Vol. 69 (July 7, 1958).

Capek, Karel. *R. U. R.* [Rossum's Universal Robots], in Tucker, Samuel M. (ed.), *Twenty-five Modern Plays.* New York: Harper & Row, 1948.

Carson, Rachel. *Silent Spring.* Boston: Houghton Mifflin, 1962.

Carter, G. C. *A Hundred Years of Evolution.* New York: Macmillan, 1957.

Clarke, Arthur C. *The Promise of Space.* New York: Harper & Row, 1968.

————. *Voices From the Sky.* New York: Harper & Row, 1965.

————. "The Evolutionary Cycle From Man to Machine," *Industrial Research Magazine,* Vol. 3 (November 1961).

————. *Interplanetary Flight.* New York: Harper & Row, 1960.

Bibliography

————. *The City and the Stars.* New York: Harcourt Brace Jovanovich, 1956.

————. *The Exploration of Space.* New York: Harper & Row, 1951.

Crow, James F. "Ionizing Radiation and Evolution," *Scientific American,* Vol. 201 (September 1959).

Darlington, Cyril Dean. *The Evolution of Man and Society.* New York: Simon and Schuster, 1969.

————. "The Origin of Darwinism," *Scientific American,* Vol. 200 (May 1959).

————. *The Evolution of Genetic Systems.* New York: Basic Books, 1958.

Davis, Kingsley. "Population Policy: Will Current Programs Succeed?" *Science,* Vol. 158 (November 10, 1967).

Day, Lincoln and Alice. *Too Many Americans.* Boston: Houghton Mifflin, 1964.

Darwin, Charles. *The Origin of Species* and *The Descent of Man.* New York: Modern Library (n.d.).

Darwin, Charles Galton. *The Next Million Years.* Garden City, N.Y.: Doubleday, 1952.

de Santillana, Giorgio, and von Dechend, Hertha. *Hamlet's Mill.* Boston: Gambit, 1969.

Dobzhansky, Theodosius. "Changing Man," *Science,* Vol. 155 (January 27, 1967).

————. *Mankind Evolving.* New Haven, Conn.: Yale University Press, 1962.

————. *Evolution, Genetics and Man.* New York: Wiley, 1958.

Dunn, L. C., and Dobzhansky, Theodosius. *Heredity, Race and Society.* New York: Mentor Books, 1957.

Durant, Will C. *Our Oriental Heritage. The Story of Civilization.* Vol. I. New York: Simon and Schuster, 1935.

Eiseley, Loren. *The Firmament of Time.* New York: Atheneum, 1960.

————. *The Immense Journey.* New York: Random House, 1957.

Enke, Stephen. "Birth Control for Economic Development," *Science,* Vol. 164 (May 16, 1959).

Ford, Amasa B. "Casualties of Our Times," *Science,* Vol. 167 (January 16, 1970).

Forster, E. M. *The Eternal Moment and Other Stories.* New York: Harcourt, Brace & World, 1928.

Freud, Sigmund. *Civilization and Its Discontents.* Joan Riviere (trans.). Garden City, N.Y.: Anchor Books, n.d.

Gamow, George. *The Creation of the Universe.* New York: Mentor Books, 1957.

Gilula, Marshall F., and Daniels, David N. "Violence and Man's Struggle to Adapt," *Science,* Vol. 164 (April 25, 1969).

Griffin, Donald R. "More About Bat 'Radar,'" *Scientific American,* Vol. 199 (July 1958).

Haldane, J. B. S. *The Causes of Evolution.* Ithaca, N.Y.: Cornell University Press, 1966.

————. "On Being the Right Size," in Newman, James R. (ed.), *The World of Mathematics.* New York: Simon and Schuster, 1956. II: 952–957.

Hall, Edward T. *The Hidden Dimension.* Garden City, N.Y.: Doubleday, 1966.

Handler, Philip (ed.). *Biology and the Future of Man.* New York: Oxford University Press, 1970.

Hardin, Garrett. "The Tragedy of the Commons," *Science,* Vol. 162 (December 13, 1968).

————. *Nature and Man's Fate.* New York: Holt, Rinehart and Winston, 1959.

Heilbroner, Robert. *The Future as History.* New York: Harper & Row, 1961.

Heyerdahl, Thor. *Aku-Aku: The Secret of Easter Island.* Chicago: Rand McNally, 1958.

Hoagland, Hudson, and Burhoe, Ralph W. *Evolution and Man's Progress.* New York: Columbia University Press, 1962.

Horowitz, N. W. "The Search for Extra-Terrestrial Life," *Science,* Vol. 151 (February 18, 1966).

Hoyle, Fred. "Forecasting the Future," in Hutchings, Edward (ed.), *Frontiers in Science.* New York: Basic Books, 1958.

————. *Frontiers of Astronomy.* New York: Harper & Row, 1955.

Hutchings, Edward (ed.), *Frontiers in Science.* New York: Basic Books, 1958.

Huxley, Aldous. *Brave New World Revisited.* New York: Harper & Row, 1958.

Bibliography

————. *Brave New World.* New York: Doubleday, 1932.

Huxley, Julian. *Man in the Modern World.* New York: Mentor Books, 1955.

————. *Evolution in Action.* New York: Harper & Row, 1953.

Jeans, James. *The Mysterious Universe.* New York: Macmillan, 1930.

Kahn, Herman, and Wiener, Anthony J. *The Year 2000.* New York: Macmillan, 1967.

Kettlewell, H. B. D. "Darwin's Missing Evidence," *Scientific American,* Vol. 200 (March 1959).

Kline, Morris. *Mathematics in Western Culture.* New York: Oxford University Press, 1953.

Kuiper, Gerard P. "Origin, Age, and Possible Ultimate Fate of the Earth," in Bates, D. R. (ed.), *The Earth and Its Atmosphere.* New York: Basic Books, 1957.

LaBarre, Weston. *The Human Animal.* Chicago: University of Chicago Press, 1954.

Landers, Richard R. *Man's Place in the Dybosphere.* Englewood Cliffs, N.J.: Prentice-Hall, 1967.

Laplace, Pierre Simon. *A Philosophical Essay on Probabilities.* Truscott, F. W. and Emory, F. L. (trans.). New York: Dover, 1951.

Lederberg, Joshua. "Experimental Genetics and Human Evolution," *American Naturalist,* Vol. 100 (September-October 1966).

Leonard, Jonathan Norton. *Flight Into Space.* New York: Modern Library, 1957.

Ley, Willy. *Rockets, Missiles and Space Travel.* New York: Viking, 1957.

Lorenz, Konrad. *On Aggression.* New York: Harcourt Brace Jovanovich, 1963.

Malthus, Thomas Robert. *An Essay on the Principle of Population, As It Affects the Future Improvement of Society.* New York: Dutton, 1914.

Medawar, P. B. *The Future of Man.* New York: Basic Books, 1961.

Moody, Paul Amos. *Genetics of Man.* New York: Norton, 1967.

More, Thomas. *Utopia.* Princeton, N.J.: Van Nostrand, 1947.

Morris, Desmond. *The Naked Ape.* New York: McGraw-Hill, 1967.

Moskowitz, Sam. *Seekers of Tomorrow.* New York: Ballantine, 1957.

Muller, Herbert J. *The Children of Frankenstein.* Bloomington, Ind.: Indiana University Press, 1970.

Muller, Hermann J. *Genetics, Medicine and Man.* Ithaca, N.Y.: Little & Snyder, 1947.

―――. *Out of the Night: A Biologist's View of the Future.* New York: Vanguard, 1935.

Mumford, Lewis. *Technics and Civilization.* New York: Harcourt Brace Jovanovich, 1963.

Newman, James R. (ed.). *The World of Mathematics.* 4 vols. New York: Simon and Schuster, 1956.

Odum, Eugene P. "The Strategy of Ecosystem Development," *Science,* Vol. 164 (April 18, 1969).

Opik, Ernst J. "The Climate and the Changing Sun," *Scientific American,* Vol. 198 (June 1958).

Ortega y Gasset, José. *Revolt of the Masses.* New York: Norton, 1957.

―――. *Toward a Philosophy of History.* Helene Weyl (trans.). New York: Norton, 1941

Orwell, George. *Nineteen Eighty-Four.* New York: Harcourt Brace Jovanovich, 1963.

Owen, Tobias. "The Atmosphere of Jupiter," *Science,* Vol. 167 (March 27, 1970).

Pascal, Blaise. *Pensées.* W. F. Trotter (trans.). New York: Random House, 1941.

Payne-Gaposchkin, Cecilia. *Stars in the Making.* Cambridge, Mass.: Harvard University Press, 1952.

Penrose, L. S. "Self-Reproducing Machines," *Scientific American,* Vol. 210 (February 1964).

Pierce, William H. "Redundancy in Computers," *Scientific American,* Vol. 210 (February 1964).

Pfeiffer, John. *The Changing Universe.* New York: Random House, 1936.

Platt, John. "What Must We Do," *Science,* Vol. 166 (November 28, 1969).

Ryan, Cornelius (ed.). *Across the Space Frontier.* New York: Viking, 1952.

Seidenberg, Roderick. *Post-historic Man.* Chapel Hill: University of North Carolina Press, 1950.

Bibliography

Sherrington, Charles. *Man on His Nature.* Garden City, N.Y. Anchor Books, 1955.

Shklovskii, I. S., and Sagan, Carl. *Intelligent Life in the Universe.* San Francisco: Holden-Day, 1966.

Simpson, George Gaylord. "The Biological Nature of Man," *Science,* Vol. 152 (April 27, 1966).

————. *This View of Life.* New York: Harcourt Brace Jovanovich, 1964.

Snow, C. P. *The Search.* New York: Scribner, 1934.

Spengler, Oswald. *The Decline of the West.* 2 vols. New York: Knopf, 1932.

Sullivan, Walter. *We Are Not Alone.* New York: McGraw-Hill, 1964.

Tax, Sol (ed.). *Evolution After Darwin: The University of Chicago Centennial.* 3 vols. Chicago: University of Chicago Press, 1960.

Teilhard de Chardin, Pierre. *The Phenomenon of Man.* New York: Harper & Row, 1959.

Thompson, D'Arcy Wentworth. *On Growth and Form.* Cambridge, Eng.: Cambridge University Press, 1961.

Thomson, George Paget. *The Foreseeable Future.* Cambridge, Eng.: Cambridge University Press, 1955.

Toulmin, Stephen, and Goodfield, June. *The Discovery of Time.* New York: Harper Torchbooks, 1965.

Toynbee, Arnold J. *A Study of History.* 12 vols. London: Oxford University Press, 1948–1961.

Turing, A. M. "Can A Machine Think?" in Newman, James R. (ed.) *The World of Mathematics,* New York: Simon & Schuster, 1956. IV: 2099-2123.

Urey, Harold C. *The Planets: Their Origin and Development.* New Haven, Conn.: Yale University Press, 1952.

Vercors. *You Shall Know Them.* Boston: Little, Brown, 1953.

Vogt, William. *People!: Challenge to Survival.* New York: Duell, Sloane & Pearce, 1948.

von Neumann, John. "The General and Logical Theory of Automata," in Newman, James R. (ed.), *The World of Mathematics.* New York: Simon and Schuster, 1956. IV: pp. 2070–2098.

Wells, H. G. *The Outline of History.* Garden City, N.Y.: Doubleday, 1961.

————. *The Time Machine.* New York: Random House, 1931.

————. *Men Like Gods.* New York: Macmillan, 1923.

White, Lynn, Jr. "The Historical Roots of our Ecologic Crisis," *Science,* Vol. 155 (March 10, 1967).

Whitehead, Alfred North. *Adventures of Ideas.* New York: Mentor Books, 1958. (a)

————. *Science and the Modern World.* New York: Mentor Books, 1958. (b)

————. *Dialogues.* Boston: Little, Brown, 1954.

Woodwell, George M. "Toxic Substances and Ecological Cycles," *Scientific American,* Vol. 216 (March 1967).

Wynne-Edwards, V. C. "Population Control in Animals," *Scientific American,* Vol. 211 (August 1964).

Young, Louise B. (ed.). *Population in Perspective.* New York: Oxford University Press, 1968.

Index